The
Japanese
Picture
Book

The Japanese Picture Book

A Selection from the Ravicz Collection

HARRY N. ABRAMS, INC., PUBLISHERS, NEW YORK

Editor: Sharon AvRutick
Designer: Ana Rogers

Library of Congress Cataloging-in-Publication Data

Hillier, Jack Ronald.
The Japanese picture book: a selection from the Ravicz
Collection/ by Jack Hillier.
p. cm.
Includes bibliographical references.
ISBN 0-8109-3503-1
1. Illustrated books — Japan — Bibliography — Catalogs.
2. Ravicz, Robert — Library — Catalogs.
3. Illustration of books — Japan. 4. Japan — Imprints.
I. Title.
Z1023.H65 1991
015.52 — dc20   91–10156
CIP

Printed and bound in Japan

All photographs by Richard Todd, except for
page 46, by Victor Pustai

Excerpt from "Little Gidding" from COLLECTED POEMS
1909–1962 by T. S. Eliot, copyright 1936 by Harcourt Brace
Jovanovich, Inc., copyright ©1964 by T. S. Eliot, reprinted by
permission of the publisher

Page 2: Plate 67; Page 3: Plate 75

CONTENTS

FOREWORD

On a short visit to Tokyo in 1968, my mother, my son Rick, and I wandered into the upstairs gallery of Isseido Bookshop. We were shown a three-volume set of books illustrating many different subjects—people, daily events, houses, trees—but in each the focus was on a varying view of the mountain Fuji. The merchant told us that the pictures were printed from woodblocks, and we noted the black and white and the intermediate shadings that characterize the intricate work of the printer. That set of *One Hundred Views of Fuji* by the artist Hokusai was my introduction to the intriguing world of Japanese picture books. Why did I buy it? There seems to be no clear explanation. Perhaps it was simply the attraction of the book format.

I was vaguely aware of the existence of Japanese woodblock prints, but I had no particular interest in the field. If art were a portion of my inventory of data about the world, it occupied restricted space, nurtured young during outings to Paris museums with Mother, who spoke to my brother Richard and me mainly about Cézanne—who better? Later, in Mexico City, the lithographs were appealing, but only in the abstract; I was more impressed by the sociopolitical stance of the artists, and I remember Mother talking to Diego Rivera, who was working on a mural in the Zócalo.

My formal education never included a course in art history. As a professional anthropologist, I was taught that collecting anything, especially in the field, was an absolute no-no, unethical, taboo—an edict I strictly followed. Curiously, I seemed to lack even the awareness of art as a part of culture. When watching a Mixtec mother decorate a pot she had fashioned, I thought of potsherds.

From the late sixties, travels to Laos, Cambodia, and elsewhere in Asia—especially India—provided me with direction for research and information for use in the university classroom. Occasionally, objects of ethnographic or other aesthetic interest would catch my eye, and in an informal, undirected way I began to acquire them. Stir in some Pop and Minimal. Their infusion into the household scene seemed quite a natural occurrence. The result? A mélange with visual and conceptual interest for us and our friends and educational breadth for our offspring, the occasional meeting place for interested others.

An economist-acquaintance hewing to an outmoded, restrictive idea questioned such accumulation by me, an academician. On another occasion, a longtime friend and colleague of mine who visited snapped, "A collector!" with finality; our contact has never resumed. But James Cahill and Stephen Addiss, the redoubtable scholars of the history of East Asian art (and collectors of paintings and Japanese picture books), have spoken to the opposite view, saying that there is nothing at all wrong with academics collecting. Charles Darwin, frustrated in the 19th century, today would undoubtedly explore methods for conjoining art and science and for explaining their apparent inherent opposition.

To me, "collecting" implies orientation and direction, methodical movement toward a goal. Such was not part of my thinking even as late as 1978, by which time nearly half of our present holdings were in hand. In Holland early that year, the gentlemanly collector Heinz Kaempfer told me of the forthcoming London sale of the Holloway Collection. I remember how exciting the news seemed, and I remember my surprise at my own excitement. (Such surprise has since disappeared, replaced by a pragmatic directness, but excitement and anticipation remain, whether the opportunity is to acquire another book or to view those in a museum or personal collection.)

Fortunate to acquire several items in the sale—especially Aoi Shūho's scintillating, droll *Kishi empu* and other examples as well—I realized that my anticipatory excitement was akin to the feelings one has when approaching a rite of passage. (I have experienced other "highs" since then, notably in addressing aspects of the books before the Ukiyo-e Society in New York and a British Library colloquium. Comfortable as a collector, I still feel adolescent in knowledge, and my participation in those coming-of-age venues has quite astonished me.)

Thenceforth, the collecting took off. My ever-supportive brother had a large hand in that expansion, urging that I investigate *ukiyo-e*; if the woodblock prints were of such note — everyone knows about them, he argued — there must be interesting book art of that class, as well. He prevailed, and my road reached out to include Utamaro, Kunisada, and others.

The growing number of books had seemed merely additive, but my interest became more intense and focused. My admiration grew for the designs, and I could only wonder at the exquisiteness of the printing and the intricacy involved in cutting the blocks; today those aspects still seem surpassing. I was always fascinated by the varied subject matter of the books — how the Japanese culture unfolds through depiction of childbirth, poetry, implements, house building, living arrangements, body language, dress, physiognomy, marriage, food preparation, festivals, specialized social groupings, eroticism, naturescapes, travel, humor, and stylized theater. It is unlikely that there exists such an extensive database of ethnographic data in graphic art form for any other culture. So as Topsy, I began to want to develop a study collection to attempt to order the variety.

My predilection has always been for wide-ranging coverage in style, artist, and content, with high-quality condition and impression an absolute requirement. I also prefer complete sets of multiple-volume books. Scholars do not always demand good condition, as they emphasize text, poem, period, style, or artist. (One once said to me "Condition doesn't matter at all." He was selling me something; I did not buy.) The twin goals of high quality and wide variety do not require that every book be "important": There are so many delightful picture books by second-rank artists, unknowns, and amateurs; rarish items in small editions commissioned by individuals or poetry societies; and limited imagery but of superior quality by those, such as Bōsai or K. Masanobu, better known for their literary achievements.

Inevitably, I am swayed from my strict adherence to these criteria. The collection contains a few incomplete sets, their rarity or attractiveness overcoming other considerations. Condition and impression are not of the finest in a few items dating from my early, learning years, from occasionally buying blind or, again, because of the temptation deriving from the rarity of some books. Item: From a wish list of eighteen I compiled twenty years ago, only five have been deleted. *Ubi sunt?* The omission of some accepted major works that have been available in the marketplace is due to my personal taste or to my opinion that the collection does not require everything in order to establish its quality and value for enjoyment, study, and research. It was gratifying to have the opinion of the highly regarded expert in Edo painting, Professor Nobuo Tsuji of Tokyo University: On viewing the collection, he remarked that it has no equivalent in size, accessibility, or condition in one place in Japan.

Chance has also played a role: I have been able to find the missing volume for two different sets and, inside-straightly, the middle volume of a three-volume set. Unexpectedly, in another case, I discovered that the mere two volumes of the *Bijutsu sekai* given in Charles Mitchell's masterful *Biobibliography* form part of a twenty-five-volume series, which I have been able to piece together during several years from sales or dealers in New York, Paris, San Francisco, and London.

But naivete and prissy selectivity have not been absent from my makeup. Fifteen years ago, two of the items on my wish list were offered to me, but I turned them down because one lacked a volume, the other a few images. (I decline to name the books through Grand Shame.) Neither will ever surface again, I fear, in any form. It was my good fortune, on the other hand, to procure quite a good example of one of the loveliest of all the books, *Suiseki gafu nihen* (1820) by Satō Suiseki, to replace another, somewhat worn and lacking in a few images; but trading up is ordinarily difficult in this field.

Repeatedly viewing images in the books has increased my ability to distinguish schools and styles, if not always the technique of individual artists, but even scholars stumble occasionally on that quest. With research taking me to India in 1981, my wife-colleague, Marilyn (whose perceptive eye and enthusiasm for this art — once she became convinced my feelings for the collection were not as strong as those for her — have served to teach me and stimulate my interest), agreed to bid on an attractive item at a forthcoming sale. The unsigned book in question was represented by the auction house expert as being an Utamaro, and Marilyn was able to acquire it through her good judgment (translation: going higher than the estimate as the bidding increased) and perseverance (ditto). A year later, in perusing the work of a Japanese scholar wherein this book was illustrated, I noted the designs were attributed to Choki, a fine printmaker whose works are few and highly prized. I was quite pleased, having no previous example of his work. Then, in 1983, further study initiated by Jack Hillier suggested that the illustrations were actually done by Hokusai. I remain interested and comfortably detached.

Familiarity — or the lack thereof — with the Japanese language fortuitously afforded me access to a grand prize: The incomparable *Taigadō gafu*. I was offered the book in 1980 by a London dealer who had located it in Japan. He agreed to allow me to peruse it during the two days prior to the reception at the British Museum celebrating the exhibition of picture books it had wisely acquired from the Jack Hillier Collection. The glow I felt from the Taiga imagery was, if possible, heightened by Hillier's response when he saw the book. I gave the dealer a check at the opening. Years later, I still see the set face and anxious eyes of another collector standing nearby. When the book had been offered to him earlier, he had turned it down, misunderstanding the title as *Gahō*, another of Taiga's works, already in his collection. *Tant pis.*

Not the least attraction of my affair with these books has been the search. Europe — London principally, but also Paris and Cologne — continues to be the main source of books from collections developed in the 19th century; sales are held also in New York and Tokyo. Working with dealers leads one further afield. Since a dealer could not make a living by selling these rare picture books exclusively, one visits dealers who market Japanese woodblock prints in general.

Once, my son Tanyo (who has graced some voyages, and his presence and eye have proved positive amulets more than once) and I were led into a bank vault in Paris to acquire two books, one, the fine Moronobu *shunga*. Why a bank vault? Presumably to justify the high price being asked.

From the same dealer, two years later, I would purchase the fabulous *Momoyo-gusa* by Kamisaka Sekka, again at a wrenching cost. Its provenance? It had been in the possession of a photographer-friend of the dealer's wife.

And more recondite sources: Tanyo spied a book among a large lot on the floor of a Los Angeles shop that specializes in Western theater books. We found another — a wonderful copy of the Falcon Feather edition of Hokusai's *One Hundred Views* that had been in the collection of the Frenchman Louis Gonse — at a dealer's in Oslo.

Early in 1983, a private dealer in Switzerland informed me that that summer he would have available a book we had discussed the previous year. He specified the date, the price, and the currency. My daughter, Simone, embarking on the obligatory backpack tour of the Greek islands and elsewhere after her junior year, deigned to meet me in Geneva for an auto tour. After noon one day we reached the dealer's steeply perched mountain home by funicular and a short walk. He produced the book — my excitement must have been apparent — and I brought out the payment. Feigning ignorance, he asked what it was for; he was planning, after all, to show the book to various people and then accept the highest bid. Perhaps I should not have been astonished, as horror stories of his dealings abound. What is the word: Outrage? He was too old for sleaze.

Still, the search has afforded me much interest, pleasure, and surprise that there is so much in so small. Sharing the books with others has proved most rewarding of all. Early on, I had no idea of their interest for scholars, but many have come to visit, and I have profited greatly from knowing them and their students and learning of their concerns. Jack Hillier — extraordinary person — has always been generous with his time and knowledge, eager to discuss the books, answer my questions, clarify the road with his monumental expertise and enthralling enthusiasm. It's been quite a trip.

ROBERT RAVICZ

INTRODUCTION

This book has a great deal to do with the activity of collecting, as well as the art of the Japanese book, and demonstrates how collecting, if intelligent, is a practical means of improving one's knowledge, of sharpening one's appreciation, of achieving connoisseurship, and even of highlighting some aspects of world art hitherto unexplored.

Dr. Robert Ravicz, to introduce him with his full name, to be shortened to R. henceforth, is, as befits a professor of anthropology, sociology, and like humanities, a student of the pictorial and plastic arts. Before becoming involved with Japanese graphics, he had acquired significant specimens of the art of India and of Mexico, as well as of Europe and America. How was the Japanese phase initiated?

Certainly, before, say, 1972, the literature on Japanese books was unlikely to impinge on even an omnivorous reader in the arts of the world: Japanese painting itself had been little written about, and typical books were those pioneering the subject (like Louis Gonse's remarkable attempt to grapple with it as long ago as 1883) or the later classroom-lecture kind of introduction, factual but hardly inspiring (such as Robert Paine's *The Art and Architecture of Japan*, 1955, with Alexander Soper). On the other hand, Japanese *prints,* of one particular school only, had a fairly voluminous literature, from treatises of the widest coverage to catalogues of individual collections, and as a consequence, most people drawn to Japanese art at all made their initial contacts through broadsheets of the Ukiyo-e, or "Floating World," school, and more often than not, made no attempt at a deeper penetration.

In fact, going back to the illustrated books of Japan, in 1968, when R. first turned his eyes in their direction, there was only one book in English of a general nature, published in 1924, and in a format, in a limited edition, and at a price that ensured that its circulation would be small and hardly likely to encompass the public libraries. This book was written by Louise Norton Brown and published in London; its title: *Block Printing and Book Illustration in Japan from the Earliest Period to the Twentieth Century.* Anyone who has in any way become involved with Japanese books has felt a debt of gratitude to the writer, about whom, astonishingly, so few facts are known. In her preface, she expressed her hope "by means of this book, to hand on to other collectors information which I had to dig out, bit by bit, slowly and laboriously, and patch together." Bearing in mind the enormity of the task of imposing some sort of chronology on lengthy lists of artists and of countless books published over four centuries — something, moreover, which not even the Japanese had attempted — one can only marvel at what she accomplished.

Apart from Mrs. Brown's book, there were a few catalogues of individual collections, among which the best are Théodore Duret's 1900 catalogue of the books that he had donated to the Bibliothèque Nationale in Paris and Kenji Toda's of 1940 of the Ryerson books bequeathed to the Art Institute of Chicago; and, in 1977, came David Chibbett's *The History of Japanese Printing and Book Illustration,* an admirably full account of printing but a rather perfunctory résumé on book illustrations. But although these publications were valuable as reference material to those already steeped in the subject, the lack of anything like adequate illustration in all (as, indeed, in Mrs. Brown's book) gave little visual proof of the great graphic art abounding in Japanese books, and so failed to encourage a specific focus of interest on the part of those attracted to Japanese art in general. Charles Mitchell's remarkable *Biobibliography* (1) has to be interposed here because, although poorly served by thumbnail reproductions, it did provide, for the first time, in 1972, complete bibliographical descriptions of each book catalogued and so became for would-be collectors a means of checking acquisitions against reliably researched specimens.

---

1. C. H. Mitchell with the assistance of Osamu Ueda: *The Illustrated Books of the Nanga, Maruyama, Shijo and Other Related Schools of Japan: A Biobibliography.* 1972

The introduction of Japanese pictorial and graphic art came to Westerners largely via woodblock prints of the Ukiyo-e school in separate sheet form, generally color prints of the late 18th to the late 19th century. This was the easiest access, due to a number of causes: the low esteem in Japan of the so-called Floating World school of painting, and especially its prints, rated simply as woodcut reproductions; in consequence, the immense quantities of prints available, compared to the paintings; the easier assimilation by Westerners of the school's genre subject matter, its quasi-realistic treatment more akin to Western style than native styles derivative from China, and even the result, as I believe, to some extent of 16th- and 17th-century European influence; and, finally, the collectibility of the prints because of their accessibility and availability (at least in the pioneer days), their appeal to mere collectors. But the books and albums containing equally valid prints — including those of Ukiyo-e artists as well as those of all other schools—for many decades had no corresponding following.

Introductory though these remarks are, they do have a bearing on the formation of R.'s collection. He came to Japanese art already a mature student of the painting and sculpture of many nations, and his instinct was to go to the heart of the matter by studying those artists whom, he analyzed, would most closely represent the quintessential style of Japan—followers of the schools that derived from and based their styles on the painters of China. And so, contrary to the normal antecedent approach, R. made his first contact with Japanese art through books containing prints by artists of the Nanga school, and a short digression is needed here to situate not only Nanga, but the other predominant schools of Japanese painting, something needed in any case to clarify the classification of books under the headings of those schools.

Brushwork for its own sake we may feel is a modern Western concept: in so thinking we would display the usual condescension, not to say arrogance, with which for so long the West has treated Oriental painting. Yet, from the earliest times—when in Europe artists were painfully struggling to represent realistically above all the forms of men and women—Chinese artists were reducing landscapes to philosophic abstractions and giving human beings their true insignificance in the scheme of things. Painting and sculpture came to Japan from China and Korea in the 6th century A.D., and in the next few centuries it is difficult to distinguish Japanese painting from that of the mainland. There was an upsurge of national literature from the 10th century on—11th-century court life was marvelously captured by the woman writer Murasaki Shikibu in the *Genji monogatari* (*The Tale of Genji*), and there began about the same time the rise of an indigenous form of painting, to be called Yamato-e, *Yamato* meaning "Our Native Land," and *e*, "Picture." Appropriately enough, the scroll illustrations of *The Tale of Genji* are the most renowned of all Yamato-e, though anonymous, like the majority of paintings of this early period. The Yamato-e scrolls, at their zenith in the 11th to 14th centuries, are marked by a naturalism and narrative raciness that are singularly Japanese, and the actual brush style is recognizably distinct from the Chinese.

Chinese influence did not end with the coming of Yamato-e, and the story of Japanese painting from then on revolves around the ascendancy of either China or Japan from period to period. The Muromachi and Ashikaga periods (14th to 16th centuries) saw a renaissance of Chinese-style painting, and are notable for paintings inspired by Zen, termed the world's "most irreligious religion." Many great named figures now emerge, the greatest being Sesshū, whose life spanned the 15th century, and who became the *beau idéal* of all admirers of Chinese-rooted Japanese art. From this tradition stemmed the prolific Kanō school of painting, which held sway from the 15th to the 19th century as the official, or academic, school, comprising a professional elite quite opposed to the individualistic scholar-artists of China, for whom painting was a way of life, not a means of making a living.

In the Momoyama period (1568–1615), the native genius for decor suddenly blossomed, given its chance in the splendid castles that were being built, largely by the Tokugawa clan that was to rule Japan from 1616 until the restoration of the Emperor in 1868. The gorgeous screens and wall paintings of such artists as Eitoku, Tōhaku Yūshō, and others are among the unique achievements of Japanese painting, and possibly the country's greatest contribution to world art.

During the latter part of the period, the Portuguese were in Japan, preaching Christianity and introducing Western art, with curious side effects on Japanese painting, in the so-called Namban screens depicting foreigners in extravagant maritime costume pieces and, even more, in paintings aping European historical and warlike compositions. Rare specimens are in the Kobe Museum, miraculous survivals despite the pogroms launched against

Christianity and everything Western associated with it, that ended the precarious tolerance of foreigners by the Japanese from the mid-16th century until the early years of the 17th century.

In the 17th century, too, the tradition of rich pattern was reinforced in numerous fields of pictorial and applied arts. In painting, it was due principally to Honami Kōetsu and Nonomura Sōtatsu, both of whom were not merely outstanding decorators in scroll or screen, but who inspired printed books which, for the first time in the world, were designed from cover to cover, text and decor, as individual works of art. (They are known as *Kōetsu-bon,* "Kōetsu books.")

The inheritor of this by-now-strong decorative tradition was Ogata Kōrin (1658–1716), whose great reputation rests largely on his originality in creating paintings based on natural forms, but with nature modified or distorted to an extent which brings them close to willful abstractions. In the early 19th century, Nakamura Hōchū, a latter-day admirer, revived the style, and in his *Kōrin gafu* of 1802 gave a prismatic intensification of Kōrin's idioms (see Nos. 92–95).

Stirrings of the birth of a new form of native painting became evident in the late 16th century when portraits of beautiful, bedizened women and screens depicting outdoor activities, cherry-viewing picnics, or field sports found favor with a growing leisure class. This partiality towards paintings of a worldly or slightly illicit slant grew rapidly with the rise of a parvenu class in Edo (Tokyo), the brash newly founded capital of the ruling Tokugawa faction. By the mid-17th century it had led to what amounted to a "people's art," purveying paintings and woodcut prints in book form for a society of literate commoners (and some of more exalted station) whose hedonistic tastes were for the ultrafashionable, the ephemeral, the scandalous. The school earned the sobriquet Ukiyo-e, the Floating World, a name connoting both gloomy Buddhistic forebodings and carefree enjoyment of the transient, the passing show.

In the 18th century, there was a fresh wave of enthusiasm for Chinese culture, resulting in a new form of painting known as Nanga, "Southern painting," a name underlining the deference to Chinese styles more sympathetic to Japanese taste than the more linear, stronger-colored Northern style. Nanga artists followed the leads of individualists in China and, in contrast especially to the official Kanō school, emulated the non-professional scholar-artist idioms of their models, developing a free, expressionistic kind of painting, notable for the lawlessness in brush mannerisms.

Somewhat later, though still in the 18th century, two great artists, Maruyama Ōkyo (1733–1795), who spearheaded a return to nature, and Matsumura Goshun (1752–1811), grafting this new naturalism upon a rootstock of Nanga, produced the delightful amalgam called Shijō (meaning "Fourth Street," the location of Goshun's studio). Shijō was at its most effective until about 1850, but thereafter, in growingly less forceful technique, prevailed among both professional and amateur artists, and so popular was it with foreign visitors that it almost reached the status of export art.

Throughout all periods, whatever the predominant trends, there were nonconformist artists, independent of the rule of schools, although their earliest training may well have been in the ranks of one or another of them. Such, for instance, are the Zen calligrapher and decorator Nakamura Shōkadō; Soga Shōhaku, contemptuous of Kanō restraints; Jakuchū, so economical in his ink paintings, so gloriously extravagant in his colorful flower-and-bird compositions; Hanabusa Itchō, too robust and rumbustious for the Kanō academicians; and others who broke ranks with much intriguing effect.

The distinctions between the paintings of these varied schools were equally marked in the prints in books, and one of the pleasures of making a catholic collection is a sense of growing familiarity with these contrasting worlds, an almost automatic recognition of the features determining the classification of each newly encountered specimen. Accustomed as he was to Western illustrated books, R. was bound to note how Japanese books differed in construction, printing technique, binding, and everything else. To begin with, Japanese papers, though strong and with a surface ingratiatingly sympathetic to woodblock printing, are not opaque, and consequently allow "show-through," which meant that printing had to be limited to one side of a sheet only. This in its turn made it necessary in the makeup of a standard book for sheets to be folded in two, forming a recto and a verso, to be stitched along the free edges. Albums differed in that the sheets were not folded, and binding was achieved by attaching sheet to sheet at the outer edges, thus avoiding the central gap that the ordinary binding of folded sheets entailed. With rare exceptions up to the time when Western printing and book-binding methods were introduced (in the 1860s), woodblocks were exclusively used for printing both text and illustrations. Where illustrations stretched over two opposing pages, they had to be cut on separate blocks. Bearing in mind the intricacy of the brush-drawn text, often in highly individual or eccentric calligraphy, block-cutting was a craft calling for a skill that never ceases to astound us. Reproductive wood engraving reached a very high standard in Europe in the 19th century, but that was the result of using fine engraving tools on the end grain of the hardest of usable woods, box, whereas the Japanese relied on a knife, and cut their softer cherry woods "on the plank." Moreover, when color printing was introduced in Japan, entailing the use of multiple blocks and the need for accurate register in printing, the gap between the respective skills East and West widened considerably: the utter supremacy of the Japanese has never been in question.

The singularity of R.'s introduction to Japanese art was not without its disadvantages. With little background knowledge of a key factor — the actual paintings of Japan (and how few have had the will and the opportunities to make more than a superficial acquaintance?) — R. was bound to apply to Japanese book illustration the criteria he would normally have applied to Western books, the first of which was that the illustrations have an aesthetic appeal to him. But at the outset, he was unable to exercise that crucial choice, since he was obliged to accept what was on offer at long range. His first source of Nanga books was a dealer in Kyoto who supplied selections that consisted largely of the dullest of all Japanese books — doctrinaire treatises on how to paint in the Chinese manner, with diagrammatic outline woodcuts instructing the tyro on how to hold the brush, how typically to represent trees, with specimens of "staffage" figures that could be copied. R. was as unmoved then as he would be now by such commonplace guides, but fortunately, in these hauls of a dragnet drawn through the stock of Kyoto booksellers, who had piles of books unsold and unsellable for decades, there were a few notable catches. I will instance the impressive *Ransai gafu* (Nos. 18–19), an example of an instructional manual that is also a work of art; and the expressionistic *Taigadō gahō* (No. 7) where, through wonderfully interpretive prints, the artist was able to maintain his influence beyond the grave. To a discerning eye, the vast distance between the instructional prints of the dry pedagogue and the powerful prints of the *Taigadō* drawing book was blatantly obvious, and R. profited from this and many similar confrontations.

Although for a time R. limited his acquisitions to books of Nanga, Shijō, and allied schools, relying for factual details on Mitchell's *Biobibliography*, R.'s taste, as well as his sense of what constituted mastery, was widening, so that when, in 1980, he was able to purchase from a London dealer a copy of the supreme masterpiece of Nanga books with color prints, the *Taigadō gafu* of 1804 (Nos. 5–6 and 8), he could appraise the distance he had traveled in a relatively short time. As T. S. Eliot wrote, in another context:

> We shall not cease from exploration
> And the end of all our exploring
> Will be to arrive where we started
> And know the place for the first time.
> *(Little Gidding)*

In this limitation of his collecting field, R. was, of course, to some extent influenced by the lines Mitchell had drawn for himself. But Mitchell lived almost within walking distance of the Kanda district, center of Tokyo's booksellers, and could make weekly forays which invariably yielded a few additions to his highly specialized collection. With R. the case was different: in time, no longer relying on bulk-buying sight unseen from Japan, he had to hope for the chance surfacing of worthwhile additions in the States or Europe, either through dealers, private owners, or, more often, public auctions. His own original bias towards the so-called classical schools was undermined by temptation offered from time to time by fine books of other kinds, especially those of the Ukiyo-e and Rimpa (Decorative, or Kōrin-oriented) schools, and within a few years, he had become as eclectic, and as explorative, in his attitude to things Japanese as he was to the arts of other nations of the world. Hence, ultimately, the comprehensiveness of the Ravicz Collection, and its potential as an introduction for the uncommitted to the whole world of Japanese graphics in book and album form.

R.'s approach to collecting can thus seen to be entirely different from that of early pioneers. Before the appreciation of the apartness, and the power, of the pictorial art of Japan had dawned, Westerners collected Japanese books for the information they gave about the country and its inhabitants. The earliest substantial collections of this kind were made by Philippe von Siebold in the 1820s (now in the Rijksmuseum voor Volkenkunde in Leiden); A. E. Nordenskiöld in 1878 (now in the Royal Library, Stockholm); and William Anderson in 1882 and 1894 (now in the British Museum and British Library). Eventually, collectors of Ukiyo-e prints came to appreciate the artistry and technical accomplishment of the picture books and albums, and considerable libraries were amassed by such amateurs as Théodore Duret, Charles Gillot, Louis Gonse, Henri Vever, Émile Javal, Charles de Haviland, Ulrich Odin, and E. Gillet. The dealer Tadamasa Hayashi, based in Paris, was instrumental in securing books, as he did prints, for the avid French collectors, and the catalogue of his valedictory sale in Paris of 1902 describes a large number of illustrated books and albums of high quality. Exceptionally, a few individuals, like Odin, Gillet, and Louise Norton Brown, confined their collections to books containing prints. Many of the collections, other than those acquired by national institutions, were dispersed in auction sales in the 1920s, and most of the catalogues, compiled by an expert bibliographer, Charles Vignier, are still invaluable to the student of Japanese books. The Vever books were to a large extent dispersed in the mid-1940s, after the war, though a few of the finest figured in the London sales of 1974 and 1975.

What sort of men were they that shared this curious obsession with Japanese books? Introductions to the catalogues of some of the individual collections, whether of public libraries or auctions, provide some interesting data. Duret, for instance, was a man of wide culture with a deep knowledge of Western art. He writes of his collecting books in Japan when on a visit in 1871–2 in company with another enthusiast, M. Cernuschi, and recalls that "M. de Chassiron…who, in a memoir published in 1861, had given a few illustrations from Hokusai's works, and had not imagined that they could ever be seen as works of art; he reproduced them, in his book, under the the titles of Natural History, caricatures, customs of the country." Duret's initial interest had been stirred by books owned by Philippe Burty displayed at the 1867 Exposition Universelle in Paris, and they were in his mind while he accompanied Cernuschi on his searches for bronzes, the object of *his* visit to Japan. Duret comments on the general ignorance of book dealers and the lack of assistance they could offer. He acknowledges how much he owed to two British enthusiasts, surgeon Dr. Anderson, already cited, and the British Ambassador to Japan, E. M. Satow (who specialized in early printed books, above all the publications of the Jesuit Press, now among the treasures of the British Library).

In contradistinction, Martin A. Ryerson formed his library of Japanese books (now in the Art Institute of Chicago) not by personal foraging but by amalgamating several existing libraries. Frederick Gookin, in his introduction to the Art Institute's Ryerson catalogue, relates the acquisition of the nucleus in 1913 comprising a selection from a private library in Tokyo; the addition in 1923 of the bulk of the Fenollosa Collection (via Francis Lathrop and Hamilton Field, both artists and collectors); and in 1926, the entire collection of Mrs. Brown, including items illustrated in her book of 1924.

Charles Vignier, who, after the First World War, gave the first reliable bibliographical accounts of Japanese books in his catalogues of the sales in Paris of a number of great French collections, introduced the 1928 catalogue of the Odin sale with a brief history of the formation of the collection. In 1898, in the course of a worldwide tour, Odin felt the first stirrings of infatuation. From 1900 to 1911 he actually lived in Kyoto and became an habitué of the bookshops, bringing together, with fastidious taste, a collection that, in his own day and ever since, has been extolled as the connoisseur's ideal. He returned to France in 1911, endured the war years there, and was obliged, eventually, to sell the collection to pay for the "high cost of living."

The preface to the Louis Gonse sale catalogue of 1924 is a perceptive eulogy of the great connoisseur by two litterateurs who were also Japonistes: Raymond Koechlin and Gaston Migeon. They do not describe how Gonse brought his remarkable collection of books together, though they do comment on the outstanding number and importance of the works, their rarity, and the beauty of the impressions. One recorded incident shows the lengths to which Gonse would go to acquire the greatest books in the earliest impression and optimum condition. It concerns a transaction with the Rijksmuseum voor Volkenkunde in Leiden. Here were deposited the books brought back to Europe by Philippe von Siebold in 1830, books carefully selected by him, during his tour in Japan as medical doctor attached to the Dutch East Indies Company, to illuminate ancient and modern history, legend, social mores, all the minutiae of daily life. He naturally had an eye to illustrated books, and, even by chance, secured many of the master-pieces for his collection. Gonse had a burning desire for one of Hokusai's most sought-after books — the *Shashin gafu* (*Album of Pictures from Nature*), the first edition of which is undated, the subsequent issue having an 1819 date. The Leiden museum had copies of both from Siebold. Gonse offered the museum a considerable number of Japanese books he had "surplus to requirements" in exchange for the undated *Shashin gafu* (the Gonse books are named in documents in the museum archive), and the transaction was agreed upon. This *Shashin gafu* became lot no. 195 in the first Gonse sale of May 1924, and was described as: *Exemplaire neuf, et tel que Von Siebold l'acheta chez un libraire vers 1830. Il est contenu dans un cartonnage de la bibliothèque de Leyde, où le n° d'entrée est répété. Volume rarissime.*

Several books bearing the Gonse seal are in R.'s library, and, indeed, a number of those dispersed in other Paris sales of the 1920s are to be found on his shelves.

Since the acquisition of books dated earlier than 1900 has become more and more difficult (the year 1900 representing, in the narrow view of most of the pioneer collectors I have been discussing, the ultimate date of fine woodcut illustration), R. has greatly enlarged his area of choice by extending his interests to post-1900, or the "modern" period. Thus his books embrace not only the transitional styles of late Meiji and Taishō (say, 1900–1922) but also the advent and evolution of the Sōsaku Hanga, the "Creative Print" that exhibits Western influence and more-over challenges the avant-garde in the West for supremacy. It is in regard to these later periods that R.'s collection enlarges our view of the historical development of the art of the Japanese book. The explosive intervention of the West into Japanese affairs in 1853 and the ensuing internecine struggle for and against the cult of the West in all its manifestations militate against anything like an unbroken sequence of evolution in Japanese graphics; but the presentation of exemplars from a collection brought together by one who has a professional imperative to chronicle the outcome of the clash of different cultures allows us to draw our own conclusions as to the rewards and penalties both for the Japanese nation and its art. Regrettably, there has been insufficient space to provide any coverage of post-1945 graphics: they are too numerous and too diverse for what could only at best be a footnote.

One aspect of post-Meiji books that has been highlighted by R.'s collection is the persistence, in new forms, of the long-established Rimpa, or Decorative, style in prints that show novel deployment of artifices introduced by Kōetsu and Kōrin, or in pattern books first made ostensibly for professional designers of fabrics, ceramics, and much else, and then published simply for their own sake, in response to a demand that has its counterpart in Western taste for Morris, MacIntosh, de Morgan, Erté, and other master designers. These modern Rimpa graphics have been little published outside Japan, and the reproductions given here (Nos. 105–112) will underline how one individual's collection can widen our appreciation of the art of Japan.

Of course, no single library, whenever and however formed, can hope to cover every aspect of the art of the Japanese book, and that of R. is unquestionably deficient in certain areas. (The same could be said of the National Diet Library in Tokyo, the largest in the country.) This perforce uneven coverage has ruled out anything like a progressive, evolutionary presentation, and instead, the intention has been to illustrate a relatively small number of R.'s finest books and to situate them in the sphere of Japanese graphic art in book form. Inevitably, this will bring into discussion other major books that are not so far in the collection and great artists who did not contribute in any significant way to the printed book.

THE PLATES

1

2

PLATE 1

ANONYMOUS CHINESE ARTIST
Landscape with a Leaning Boulder
From *Hasshū gafu*
八種画譜
(*A Collection of Eight Volumes of Pictures*), vol. 7
c. 1672

We begin with a book that was not among the first to enter the collection, but was acquired only after a number of treatises on "how to paint in the Chinese manner" had taken their place on the shelves. It was the earliest compilation of prints based on Chinese originals to be produced in Japan: a series of eight volumes that acted like a lifeline thrown between the two cultures of China and Japan in the 17th century. Indeed, the volumes were founded on a set originally published in China, of which all traces except the prefaces (since they are repeated in the Japanese edition) have disappeared. The Chinese set seems to have been first published in 1621, though certain of the eight volumes had appeared earlier; and the colophon date of the last volume in the Japanese series is 1672. The Japanese set, without having an acknowledged printed title, is known as *Hasshū gafu* (*A Collection of Eight Volumes of Pictures*).

The Japanese audience for *Hasshū gafu* must have been highly cultured. There were three volumes of Tang (7th–10th centuries) poems with illustrations; a volume of the "classical" plum, bamboo, orchid, and chrysanthemum; one of flowers and birds; another of flowering plants; a volume of copies or transcripts of famous paintings; and a last volume of copies of fan paintings.

For all the sway of China over Japan in the arts since earliest times, *Hasshū gafu* was the first printed embodiment of a wide range of the pictorial art of the mentor country. Although the bare outline cuts gave little inkling of the crucial aspects of style—the nuances of tone, the individual handling of the brush—sufficient was conveyed of the impressive composition of landscapes and the imaginative juxtaposition of bird and plant to have had an influence on many Japanese aspirants to a classical Chinese manner.

The point most to remember is that this earliest widespread instruction was with woodcuts (original paintings being largely unavailable) and this woodcut source—especially in the depiction of foliage and the marking of *cun*, outlines of strata in mountain forms—continued to be revealed in Japanese painting for several centuries to come. In *Taigadō gafu* (see Nos. 5–6 and 8), one even wonders if Taiga were not patently stressing the woodcut origins of his style and making a virtue of necessity when the necessity had (by reason of color printing) virtually disappeared.

PLATE 2

ANONYMOUS CHINESE ARTIST
Lyre-Tailed Bird on a Flowering Shrub
From *Hasshū gafu,* vol. 4
八種画譜
c. 1672

By 1672, there was already a fairly strong native tradition of "bird and flower" painting in Japan, and in contrast to the landscapes, the woodcut images of this subject matter in *Hasshū gafu* were not of a kind to promote stylistic impetus. Yet they had their value, if only in introducing the Japanese to hitherto-unknown aspects of the natural world, and, of course, the albums were not produced solely as guidebooks for painters.

胡長伯畫自文五
峰入手晚乃出入
叔明子久兼筆古
質頗類文代以肯
人書學禮器碑

PLATE 3
WANG KAI (Chinese artist, dates unknown)
Landscape in Round Fan Format
From *Kaishien gaden*
芥子園画伝
(The first Japanese edition of the landscape section of the
Mustard Seed Garden Manual of Painting)
1753

Naturally, the *Hasshū gafu* volumes were not the only Chinese books of which Japanese editions were published. As regards the inculcation of Chinese styles of painting, there was no greater influence than the *Mustard Seed Garden Manual of Painting.* The volumes had been produced in China in 1679 (landscape) and 1701 (birds and flowers) and were illustrated by color prints of outstanding quality. The Japanese publishers did their best to emulate them, succeeding, in fact, in producing the first large body of woodblock color prints in Japanese book history, of immense influence on the development of Chinese-style painting and, also, on multiblock color printing.

The round fan format was common in early Chinese painting and served in a way to emphasize the abstract, nonrepresentational intent of the painting. In this case, no specific location was intended, only an essentially remote rocky waste, fit for a recluse's dwelling.

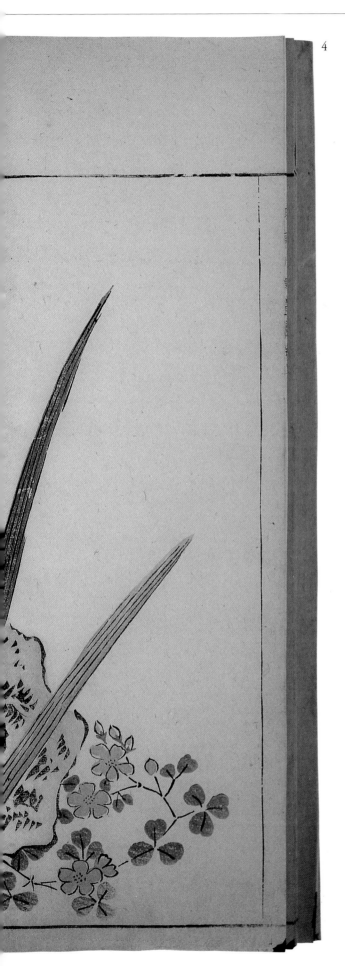

PLATE 4
ŌOKA SHUMBOKU (1680–1763)
Iris siberica
From *Minchō shiken*
明朝紫硯
(***The Purple Inkstone of the Ming Dynasty***)
Reprint of the 1746 first edition
c. 1812

Slightly earlier than the first Japanese edition of the *Mustard Seed Garden Manual of Painting* of 1748, Shumboku was commissioned to produce the *Mincho shiken*. It was based on a Chinese publication of the 17th century (all copies of which are now apparently lost, though a few of the designs are known to have been repeated in the *Mustard Seed Garden* volumes). The 1746 book is extremely rare: it was a deluxe edition, the colors being largely applied by refined stenciling, and the copy in the British Museum is known (because the cover title is lacking) by the internal title *Minchō seidō gaden* (*A Collection of Lively Ming Dynasty Drawings of Flowers and Insects*). Difficulties were clearly encountered in completing the original edition, and only two volumes of the projected three were issued in 1746, though a three-volume set appeared later, some copies being known with an 1812 date.

The Chinese artist situated his simply treated iris against the kind of weathered, perforated rock that symbolized a garden designed on philosophic lines.

5

6

7

Taigadō gahō, both published in 1804. *Taigadō gafu* contains several masterpieces of landscape in graphic art, interspersed with pages that purport to be instructional but which, like some composers' études, are of more startling originality and virtuosity than his regular pieces. This print of *Tree Forms*, for instance, utilizes all the xylographic conventions for foliage and tree structure, but simply to enhance the shimmer of line and the arabesque of forms. It is only at a second glance that we realize how non-naturalistic are the colors.

PLATE 6

IKENO TAIGA

Rounded Mountain

From *Taigadō gafu*

大雅堂画譜

1804

In this print, Taiga has confined himself to *sumi* (ink prepared for painting or printing from solidified ink sticks rubbed down with water on an ink stone and ranging in intensity from deepest black to weaker tones), only in different strengths of tone. The mountain is not presented as an identifiable topographical feature, but simply as an abstract evocation of this kind of weathered stone and an opportunity to weave clusters of strata lines into a rhythmic mass.

PLATE 7

IKENO TAIGA

Barrier Mountain

From *Taigadō gahō*

大雅堂画法

(*Taiga's Art of Painting*)

1804

By 1804, Taiga had been dead nearly thirty years, but his reputation had grown to such an extent and the enthusiasm for Chinese-style art was such that not only *Taigadō gafu* but an equally momentous three-volume work, *Taigadō gahō*, came out in the same year, from a different publisher. The *Gahō* dealt in a more systematic way than the *Gafu* with the artist's surpassing technical mastery and invention.

In the *Barrier Mountain*, the harsh reality of an alpine retreat is brought home by the severity of the bleak ink line and washes, by the glacier-scarred foreground, the stripped trees. *Taigadō gahō* presents almost an inventory of Taiga's immense resource in converting Chinese motifs and techniques into Japanese graphic art, something quite distinct from the Chinese paintings from which it derives and relying to an incalculable extent on the inspired collaboration of the printmakers, the block cutters, and printers.

PLATE 5

IKENO TAIGA (1723–1776)

Tree Forms

From *Taigadō gafu*

大雅堂画譜

(*The Drawing Book of Taiga*)

1804

Ikeno Taiga was an artist of exceptional gifts, and though it is in his landscapes that one senses the presence of Chinese elements, remembered dimly from the *Mustard Seed Garden* manual, he is a case of genius utterly transforming intractable material. He was commemorated in two wonderful books, *Taigadō gafu* and

8

PLATE 8
IKENO TAIGA
Trees by a Rocky Stream
From *Taigadō gafu*
大雅堂画譜
1804

The artist forgets his vast knowledge of the theory and practice of Chinese painting and allows the poet to prevail. He depicts a quiet, rock-guarded inlet, with old trees on the near bank and a recluse's hut by the water's edge. Everything—crumbling brush line and pale, unemphatic colors—suggests the silent, contemplative atmosphere where the literatus finds the perfect retreat. We can judge just how far artist and woodcut interpreter have surpassed any of the *Hasshū gafu* prints: it is as if warm life had been breathed into wooden stereotypes.

PLATE 9
MIKUMA KATEN (1730–1794)
Ikeno Taiga and His Wife, Gyokuran
From *Kinsei kijin den*
近世畸人伝
(*Lives of Eccentrics of Today*). First series
1790

We might wonder what manner of man was Taiga, and surprisingly there is this intimate portrait of the great artist shown making music with his devoted wife, Gyokuran. It is one of the illustrations by a fellow literatus, Mikuma Katen, *haikai* (haiku) poet and artist, for a book on the *Lives of Eccentrics of Today,* written by one Ban Kokei in 1788 and published in 1790.

Taiga and his wife were both painters and the close harmony of their lives together was renowned. Katen has captured the confusion of the room where these bohemians worked, the litter of painting utensils, the mounted pictures, the devotional sculpture on the pile of books, the poem extolling "the color of spring" open on the low table, the garden flowers intruding through the circular window. Taiga plays his antique two-stringed instrument, a *teikin,* blissfully unaware of anything save Gyokuran's accompaniment on the *chin.*

10

9

PLATE 10
YAHANTEI BUSON (1716–1783)
The Haiku Poets Keikō and Chigetsu
From *Haikai sanjū rokkasen*
俳諧三十六歌僊
(*Thirty-six Immortals of Haikai*)
1799

Yahantei Buson, as a Nanga artist, has a reputation on a par with that of Ikeno Taiga, but he was of a different caliber, and more closely approximates the character of the *bunjinga,* the literatus artist, than his more powerful contemporary. Indeed, Buson was at bottom a poet and has always been as widely respected a poet of haiku as a painter. As a painter, he was gentler, less magisterial than Taiga and tended to inspire followers who seemed not to seek worldly fame but preferred the obscurity of the recluse.

PLATE 11
KI BAITEI (1734–1810)
Porter
From *Kyūrō gafu*
九老画譜
(*The Drawing Book of Kyūrō*)
1795

As a landscapist, Baitei was clearly a disciple of Buson, decidedly Nanga, though less poetic in his handling of standard themes. In his drawings for books, but especially in his major *gafu* (literally "an album of drawings," though often an exposition of an artist's style, with an implied suggestion of instruction), where he used the art name Kyūrō, he relied on a direct brusqueness of statement that hints at a temperamental individual of an abrasive nature and a caustic wit.

The *Porter* sums up his no-nonsense attitude. This is a blunt portrayal of a menial and one has to admire the uncompromising collaboration of the woodblock carver, who conveys the artist's line and mass in all their abrupt roughness.

Buson's major paintings, sometimes in screen format, by which he is known today, were not reproduced in books during his lifetime, and it was not until 1799 that Buson's standing as an artist was more widely established by the publication of *Haikai sanjū-rokkasen*, though that was still the outcome of the vogue for his poetry.

No one expected these portraits to be speaking likenesses of the poets. Buson may have had some intention of making them recognizable, but the purposely offhand *bunjinga* style made each figure simply a calligraphic accompaniment to the dashing verse, though a subtle distinction is made in some editions by the use of inks of different strengths for the outline of the figure on the one hand, and for the calligraphy of the verses on the other. The success of this sort of drawing lies in its very non-naturalism: the *haiga*, as this combination of verse and drawing is called, is meant to be read as a single image, and a too-explicit portrait would be inimical to that intention.

11

12

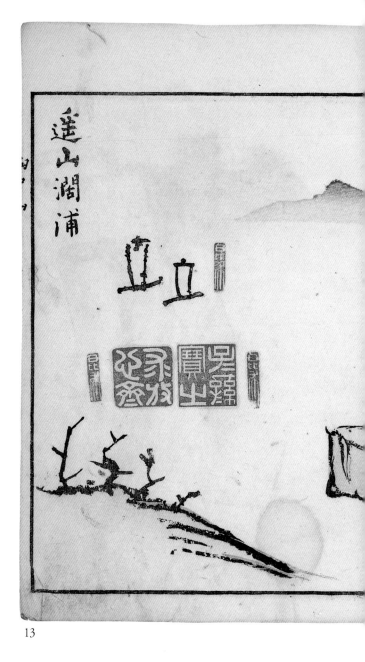

13

PLATE 12
KI BAITEI
Thatched Cottages
From *Kyūrō gafu*
九老画譜
1795

PLATES 13–14
KAMEDA BŌSAI (1752–1826)
Two landscapes from *Kyōchūzan*
胸中山
(*Mountains of the Heart*)
1816

There is even a restless acerbity about Baitei's woodcut landscapes, a spikiness in the trees that contrasts markedly with Buson's paintings of copses with vague contours of misty foliage. There is no gracious living in Baitei's world, only the harsh realities of winter, cottages hemmed in by thickets of branches as unfriendly as barbed wire.

Bōsai is an out-and-out *bunjinga* artist whose drawings are ingratiatingly easy to enjoy. These two prints are from a poetically named book — *Kyōchūzan* (*Mountains of the Heart*), so distancing itself from anything with the taint of topography and centering on those elements of grandeur, isolation, and the belittlement of man that the

14

Chinese philosopher-painters found in the mountains. Just as Buson's *haijin*, composers of *haikai* (No. 10), are imaginary portraits, so Bōsai's mountains mean nothing to alpinists, and R. found it easy to appreciate them as though they were indeed abstracts and not too far from the distorted rock formations in modern Western art, though he would be the first to warn against making too much of what is, after all, only a coincidence.

In No. 14, the inscription "Rivers and mountains are a help to me in composing poems" conveys the image of the hermit-sage of Chinese tradition, isolated in a hut anchored to a rocky outcrop in a bay; in No. 13, a similar hut is visible high on a mountainside in the far distance. A former collector with a knowledge of how the Chinese frequently desecrated their paintings with the seals of ownership has imitated the aberration by impressing a pattern of his seals in the blank area representing the bay.

The literatus style is evident in the jerky brushstrokes and the loose structure of the rocks, and gains much from the collusion of the printmakers in contriving the crayony texture of mountain forms and trees, and the restriction of colors to those in *bunjinga* effusions.

Bōsai was a more convivial fellow than his austere landscapes, peopled only by recluses and sages, might suggest. He was in frequent demand as a writer of prefaces to other artists' books, or for colophons to their paintings, and like many of his calling, had a reputation for addiction to *sake*.

寒葉齋畫譜〇卷之三

玉洞凝雪

15

PLATE 15

RYŌTAI KANYŌSAI (1719–1774)
Three Hares in the Snow
From *Kanyōsai gafu*
寒葉斎画譜
(*The Drawing Book of Kanyōsai*)
1762

Kanyōsai gafu is the earliest of a number of books designed by this artist in homage to Shen Nampin, a Chinese artist who spent some time in Japan in the 1730s, and who by his own teaching (or that of his pupils, like Kumashiro Yūhi, under whom Kanyōsai studied) created a sub-school of Nanga. Other pupils of Yūhi whose illustrated books are notable are Sō Shiseki and Ransai, and the group formed part of what is known as the School of Nagasaki, since it was to this city that Shen Nampin was, as a foreigner, confined, and where the school continued to flourish after his return to China.

Although Shen Nampin's paintings were often colorful, Kanyōsai's own versions, in painting or print, were invariably in *sumi*, but the prints in *Kanyōsai gafu* are enlivened by variations in the ink printing brought about by what, for want of an explicit native term, has been called "trituration" of the surface of the woodblock, though how this was achieved, whether by use of metal dusts or special tools, has not so far been discovered. The expedient ensured a mottled, almost mezzotint-like effect, remarkably suggestive of the sensuous warmth of brush-applied ink. Subtleties of this kind demanded unusually sympathetic interpretation on the part of the block makers, and the publishers not only of Kanyōsai but his fellow adherents to the teachings of Shen Nampin achieved a high level of consistency in exploiting this technical expedient.

Three Hares is a typical Shen Nampin subject, to which Kanyōsai has given a graphic expressiveness by isolating the winter-white animals in an area stippled with snow-covered flowers and herbage.

16

PLATE 16
SŌ SHISEKI (1712–1786)
Litchi and Bird
From *Sō Shiseki gafu*
宋紫石画譜
(*The Drawing Book of Sō Shiseki*)
1765

In the mid-18th century, color printing was still at an experimental stage. Publishers had not finally settled on the technique to be employed, and pioneer works such as Ritsuō's *Chichi-no-on* of 1734, the first Japanese versions of the *Mustard Seed Garden* of 1748 and 1753, and even the Ukiyo-e *e-goyomi,* "pictorial calendars," introduced around 1764, were to some extent experimental. Both Sō Shiseki's albums cited in this and the following item con-

tain a few examples of color printing known in the West, where it was also exploited as *à la poupée,* a method whereby all the colors were printed from a single block. The eventually established color printing procedure demanded a separate block for each color, register with the outline being achieved by a simple system of aligning each sheet progressively within a right-angle cut at one corner of each block and a borderline continuing along one side of the right-angle. In the *à la poupée* method, the colors were applied to a single block with a printer's rag dabber, and there was always a certain unpredictability as to how the colors would react under the pressure of the burnisher *(baren)* used for proofing. In most instances, the colors lying side by side tended to fuse at the edges, and the chance effects constitute one of the charms of this kind of printing. But it was obviously too unreliable for general commercial use.

画
譜

17

PLATE 17
SŌ SHISEKI
Hares
From ***Kokon gasō***
古今画藪
(*A Thicket of Ancient and Modern Pictures*)
c. 1770s

Every bibliographer of Japanese books has held up his hands in horror at the impossible tangle of books published with this title, and this is not the place to make one further attempt to impose some sort of order on the various sets, each of eight volumes, which seem to

have been drawn at random from an accumulated reservoir of different volumes. On the other hand, many unusual and inspiring prints are scattered in the volumes concerned, and R., like every other serious collector, could not avoid securing *his* set, which covers a span of years and many facets of the Shen Nampin style. It is interesting to compare Sō Shiseki's rendering of hares in the snow with Kanyōsai's (No. 15). The similarity suggests that both artists may have been interpreting an original by Shen Nampin, or, more likely, that Sō Shiseki took his cue from the Kanyōsai book. The two prints allow us to distinguish the looser handling of Kanyōsai from the more detailed, naturalistic brushwork of Sō Shiseki.

18

PLATES 18-19
MORI RANSAI (1740–1801)
Two Birds and a Flowering Plum Branch in Snow
From *Ransai gafu*
蘭斎画譜
(*The Drawing Book of Ransai*)
1802

Followers of the style of the Chinese artist Shen Nampin were fervent-ly evangelistic in preaching his style to the Japanese. Both Kanyōsai and Sō Shiseki designed *gafu* that furthered the cause, but Mori Ransai, a pupil of Yūhi who had actually had instruction from Shen Nampin himself, proved himself the most persistent. Each of his three publications, two in 1778 and a third in 1802, though with the title *Ransai gafu*, provided instructional courses founded on Shen Nampin. But each set of four volumes, one based on bamboo, the second on the epidendrum, or orchid, the third of more general coverage, devel-oping its theme from simple outlines to the most advanced and com-plex images, rises far above the level of a mere instructional manual. Ransai was an artist who made a virtue of his method, and in the final episodes of his developments, the "transcendental" of his studies, chal-lenged the printmakers to virtuoso responses.

R. is most fortunate in possessing an original brush-drawn mock-up for one volume of the 1802 set. Such a survival is almost unprecedented, but invaluable in demonstrating the problems set to the interpreters and their triumphs as revealed in the ultimate prints.

Here (below) we show the drawing for the double-page print of two birds and a snow-covered plum branch, and the actual book print based on it. Remember, the artist had at his command all the tones and halftones that the brush could deploy, while the printmak-er was confined to the impression from a single block. Admire how skillfully the block maker has conveyed the roughness of the bark and its varying tonality, and how subtly the printer has reduced the tone of the background to give weight to the branch and the aerial buoy-ancy of the bird on the wing.

19

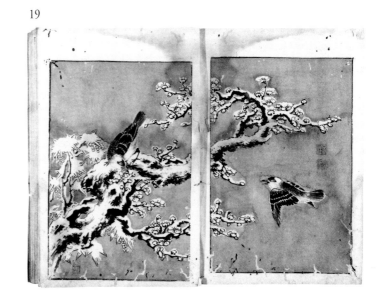

20

PLATE 20
TANI BUNCHŌ (1763–1840)
Bamboo
From *Shazanrō ehon*
写山楼画本
(*The Picture Book of Shazanrō*)
1816

Tani Bunchō was one of Japan's most gifted artists, and although quite eclectic, was fundamentally Nanga. He came of good family, was to some extent sponsored by Matsudaira Sadanobu, the prime minister, and was highly influential in spreading the Nanga precepts among artists in the Edo area. His work appears in a large number of anthologies, but his finest sustained graphic output figured in *Shazanrō ehon* (*Shazanrō* was a nom de plume) from which a characteristic specimen is illustrated.

The bamboo was a classical vehicle for exhibiting virtuosity in ink brushwork, and Bunchō challenges the Chinese masters in the print reproduced. What was looked for was not just a faithful representation of the plant but the expressiveness that the artist could project by his treatment, so that the leaves and canes were imbued with life, were bowed down by adversity, showed resilience against violence or sensuous languor under brilliant sun. The brushwork was crucial, and Bunchō here deploys all the subtle variation in tones that can be induced from the *sumi* at the hands of a master printer.

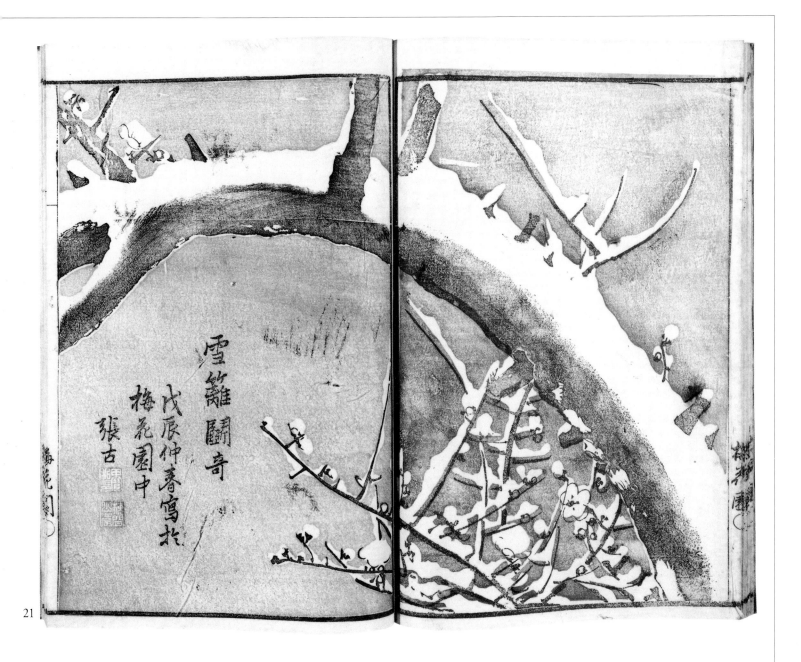

雪籬鬪奇
戊辰仲春寫於
梅花園中
張古

Plate 21
OKADA BAIKAN (1773–1849)
Plum Tree in Snow
From ***Baika-chō***
梅花帖
(***Album of Plum Blossom***)
1808

A retainer of a Nagoya *daimyō* (overlord of the region), Baikan was a poet, calligrapher, and artist with a deep-rooted obsession for plum trees, numbers of which he had planted in his garden, whence he took his art name Baika-en, "Garden of Plum Blossom."

His one picture book, *Baika-chō*, glorifies his passion and contains a number of magically romantic or dramatic variations on the theme.

The early flowering plum was ever a favorite emblem for the promise of the New Year, to the extent of almost becoming hackneyed: few artists have made so striking an image as Baikan with his great, arching snow-laden bole.

22

PLATE 22

YAMAMOTO BAIITSU (1783–1856)
Lakeside Village among Pines
From *Sanji sansui shoga jō*
三時山水書画帖
(*Album of Calligraphy and Paintings
at Three Times a Day*)
Preface dated c. 1821

Artists expressed their commitment to the Nanga philosophy in varying degrees, from vehement passion to undemonstrative compliance. Baiitsu was one of the gentler spirits, and his paintings, and the prints after his paintings, have a quiet serenity that is the reverse of the restless questing of other artists like Taiga, Gyokudō, and Mokubei.

This lakeside view is suffused with moist warmth, there are no harsh lines anywhere, the mountain forms are stippled, and the conifers are strung along the banks with broken lines that evoke a summer haze. Baiitsu excels in understatement, a reticence subtly conveyed by the *sumi* tones of this print.

23

Matsumura Goshun (1752–1811)
Chestnuts and Fungus
From an untitled anthology
1793

It is easy to understand how R., relying on Mitchell's *Biobibliography* as his first guide, came to have a leaning towards Nanga, Shijō, and other schools deriving from Chinese sources. The books so far described show how successfully R. had covered the Nanga field, though they were not acquired in the chronological order in which they are arranged here. The acquisition of Shijō-illustrated books has been even more haphazard, and it was only recently that R. acquired the 1793 album seen now as a momentous publication, akin to a dated manifesto announcing the advent of a new school of painting — Shijō. When in 1974 I wrote about the anthology in *The Uninhibited Brush,* only two copies had been described (Mitchell's,

now in the New York Public Library, and my own, now in the British Museum), but since then, three more have come to light (Museum of Fine Arts, Boston; Tenri, Nara, Japan; and R.). Only the Tenri copy has a title label, but this is hand-brushed *(Gasan-shū, Collection of Pictures and Inscriptions)* and cannot be relied on.

But it is a precious album as well as rare. Goshun rightfully takes first place as the founder of the school, and his composition of drooping leaves, chestnuts, and fungus is typically reticent and quiet. Wordless, it conveys an autumnal melancholy. It is signed Gekkei, a name Goshun often used during the period when he looked upon Buson as his mentor.

24

Plate 24
Watanabe Nangaku (1767–1813)
Woman and Maidservant Mounting a Hill
From the same untitled anthology
1793

Of the five artists who contributed to the 1793 album, only three went on to make any mark: Goshun, Nangaku, and Genki. Nangaku's print, even this early, is archetypal of the Shijō figure print, the outlines simplified, the color randomly applied and with a surprising and original touch, like the pine seen beyond the hilltop, brushed in with broad, transparent washes. In *The Uninhibited Brush,* I tried to summarize the essentials of Shijō style. "Elision, compression, lyricism, suggestionism, evocativeness: these are the qualities which, from Goshun onwards, pervade what we might, from our point of view, dismiss as impressionistic trifles." Already, in 1793, Nangaku was exemplifying this summary of attributes.

25

PLATE 25
YAMAGUCHI SOKEN (1759–1818)
Arm Pillow
From *Yamato jimbutsu gafu*
倭人物画譜
(*A Book of Pictures of Japanese People*). Part I
1800

The freedom that Nanga and Shijō artists took for granted is particularly striking in their figural works. At the turn of the 18th century, when Soken's *Yamato jimbutsu gafu* (Parts I and II) were published, departures from representationalism in Western drawings were normally only countenanced in what we now term caricatures or cartoons, such as lowlife or comic or political paintings and prints purveyed in Britain by Gillray, Rowlandson, and others of their ilk. Soken, on the other hand, had the sanction of classical Oriental tradition for his offhand depictions of the human form, and the block cutters did nothing to ameliorate the uncouthness of his brush line. Soken also designed with all the native flair for space as a vital con-

comitant. He was not afflicted with that *horror vacui* that led Western artists to overcrowd their picture space.

There had already been publications of books of contemporary genre scenes before Soken, but his two sets led to them becoming an established vehicle for Shijō artists to express themselves, their commentaries on everyday life being conveyed in the style individual to each. Soken, Nangaku, Nantei, Bumpō, Shūho, Suiseki, and Chinnen are those most successfully translated into book form; others, such as Rosetsu and Nanrei, whose album and scroll printings are so impressive, were not, to our loss, induced by publishers to design major *gafu*, though they made their mark in occasional contributions to anthologies.

The delightful *Arm Pillow* (so entitled in the "List of Contents" at the outset of Part I) is typical of the summary drawings throughout, and of the frequent playful touches, like the contented cat seated on the framework of the *kotatsu*, the charcoal brazier under the striped covering. It is wintertime, and the girl has fallen asleep, with the letter she was reading lying beside her.

26

PLATE 26
YAMAGUCHI SOKEN
Two Priests Seated under a Tree with a Samurai
From *Yamato jimbutsu gafu.* Part II
倭人物画譜
1804

The three figures under the bare tree make a powerful composition. The blossom is just budding on the plum tree, and one suspects that one of the monks is inscribing a haiku on a poem paper for the benefit of the samurai seated beside him. The second monk, no doubt a senior abbot, kneels with his head resting on a *jui,* a kind of emblem of authority.

27

Plate 27
YAMAGUCHI SOKEN (1759–1818)
Lotus
From *Soken gafu: sōka no bu*
素絢画譜草花之部
(*Book of Drawings by Soken: Plant and Flower Section*)
1806

This is a translation of an ink painting into a magnificent woodcut, where the printmaker has not merely cut the outline but has scraped the surface of the block to simulate the varying tones of the ink washes, producing a print of surprising strength and variety of texture. Several other outstanding prints in this book rely on this technique, which may not be unique to Japan but was certainly brought to its highest artistic achievement there. It was never used to heighten illusionistic effect, but rather to convey the unevenness of tone in the artist's original painting. The purely graphic enhancement was perhaps unforeseen, but in fact, properly handled, the tonal variations led to results that differed from the untouched outline print as greatly as a mezzotint from a line engraving. We do not have the original ink drawing on which the *Lotus* was based, but the print must differ from it crucially, and it is, in effect, a masterpiece in its own right in a different medium.

PLATES 28–29
AOI SHŪHO (1769–1859)
Ferry Boat and *Procession of Courtesans*
From *Kishi empu*
葵氏艶譜
(*Mr. Aoi's Chronicle of Charm*)
1803

Kishi empu, a sarcastic title capable of a number of translations, of which *Mr. Aoi's Chronicle of Charm* gives one a foretaste of the drift of the contents, is a pictorial satire of the lives of the humbler folk of Kyoto. The pungent wit of the pictures, unaccompanied by any text, is brought home by startling compositions, expressive line, and bold color printing. It is a book that has appealed more to Western taste

than Japanese, and in fact it was not until 1982 that a complete copy came to light in Japan and was then, for the first time, given critical acclaim, though it had been enjoyed in the West, where at least half a dozen copies have been located, ever since Duret's 1900 catalogue of his Japanese books in the Bibliothèque Nationale.

At the same time as the book was revealed to the Japanese as a masterpiece, the artist was established as Aoi Shūho, until then only known by the pseudonym Sōkyū cited in the preface to *Kishi empu*. Shūho was already known as the artist of another exceptional book (the *Tsuwamono zukushi*, No. 30) and of several forceful contributions to anthologies.

It is worth mentioning that R.'s copy came from another collection of note (that of Owen E. Holloway, author of *Graphic Art of Japan: The Classical School,* 1957. The collection was sold anony-

29

mously at Sotheby's in 1978, but the ownership was later revealed by comparison with reproductions in Holloway's book). No two collections could have been formed with more different aims: Holloway revered only art based on classical China and snobbishly disparaged the "popular" or, in his word, "plebeian," Ukiyo-e; R., after an early restriction to "classical" schools, developed into a collector of unrestricted eclecticism, with a breadth of view that extends to every aspect of creativeness in Japanese graphic art.

In *Ferry Boat,* Shūho shows the same sort of intensity as a German Expressionist. The men seem ungainly, even deformed, under the stress of action, the oarsman at the stern especially; and the tilt of the boat, riding the agitated waves, not only conveys the wallowing passage, but gives a disconcerting unsteadiness to the composition. The distant craft, astutely touched in, accentuate the heaving

motion of the foreground craft. Shūho achieves his effects with an intentional rejection of any refinement, either in line or color. This is *faire brutal* with a vengeance.

The *Procession of Courtesans* was one of the sights of the Shimmachi, the red-light district in Kyoto. Shūho presents it as a blaze of color, the parasols syncopating the powerful diagonal movement. But the queens of the licensed district are homely in looks under their bedizened hairdos, and the young acolytes, boys and girls, carry their balls solemnly and without playfulness. The display is conceived in an utterly different spirit from those in Edo that we view through the eyes of Utamaro or Hokusai, who portray beauties in fastidious line and color: Shūho makes no concessions, but the sweep of his great design is unmatchable.

30

PLATE 30
SAITŌ SHŪHO
Benkei and the Young Yoshitsune
From *Tsuwamono zukushi*
つはものつくし
(*An Array of Brave Warriors*)
Preface dated 1805

This is another satirical work of Shūho, mocking the heroes of legend and history, making fun of stories lying at the very heart of the Japanese worship of bravery, warlike prowess, and quixotic self-sacrifice. In his treatment of a traditional theme of prodigious infant strength, Yoshitsune is shown as a stripling testing the powers of Benkei, a standard symbol of martial ferocity, of whom Shūho gives a demeaning "backside" shot, not at all in keeping with the accepted image of a towering giant bristling with a frightful armory of weapons. Shūho contrives a dramatic composition, aided by color printing that emphasizes the diagonal movement.

PLATES 31–32
SATŌ SUISEKI (active c. 1807–1840)
Cats at a Brazier and *Flight of Birds*
From *Suiseki gafu nihen*
水石画譜二編
(*The Drawing Book of Suiseki*). Second series
1820

Suiseki's second series is, by general consent, at least of judges in the West, one of the most original and arresting of all Japanese books of prints. The first series, which appeared in 1814, comprising figure studies printed with limited color, shows Suiseki as an artist of unusual vision, but the twenty-nine bird-and-flower prints comprising the second part of a set advertised as a trilogy (landscapes were to complete the work) transcend in emotive power anything in the whole range of Japanese art in print form. They are astonishingly varied within the bounds set by the theme, exploring every possible variation in viewpoint, composition, and tempo; and they are profoundly moving, as the two examples reproduced demonstrate.

The two somnolent cats suggest a weighty largo; the *Flight of Birds* a restless, driving agitato. In each case, the forms and the colors underscore the mood: the heaviness of the brazier and the comfortable rotundity of the cats; the bright green and yellow of the birds and their surging motion.

We are readily in sympathy with Suiseki's prints because they appeal to whatever it is in us that responds to certain aspects of our own Western art in modern times: the cats are premonitory of Bonnard's lithographs; the birds in flight are so reminiscent of certain designs by E. McKnight Kauffer that you wonder whether, in fact, Suiseki's print was not familiar to him. Certainly, Suiseki is another of those artists who have been more greatly esteemed by foreigners than by the Japanese themselves: possibly we react intuitively to Suiseki's struggle "against the grain" to express himself, unlike, say, Chinnen, who wields his brush untroubled by any check to its fluency.

31

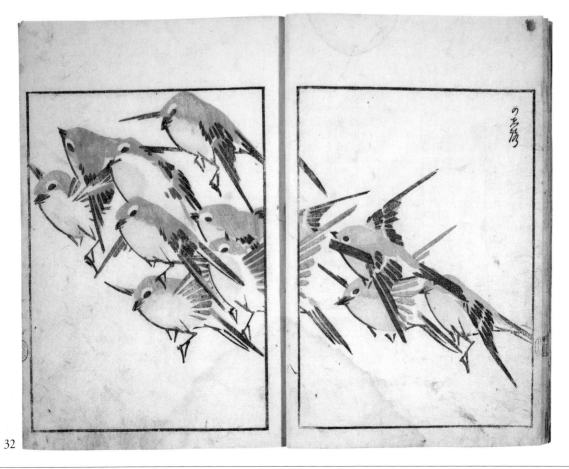

32

41

古秀画譜

33

PLATE 33
HATTA KOSHŪ (1760–1822)
Drying Fishing Nets
From *Koshū gafu*
古秀画譜
(*The Drawing Book of Koshū*)
1812

Suiseki's prints have that mysteriously moving power that leads us to think of him as a genius: almost any print from the second series could have selected itself for inclusion in this volume. Other contemporary artists are more mortal beings who only infrequently inspired or persuaded the printmakers to a compelling collusion. Such, for instance, is Hatta Koshū, who had the benefit of studying under the great Ōkyo for a time, and who developed into a thoroughly reliable painter and contributor to the major anthologies such as *Meika gafu* and *Keijō*

gaen, both of 1814, but who lacked the individuality that might have lifted his work above an unremarkable level.

But a print like *Drying Fishing Nets,* in the album devoted to his work, *Koshū gafu,* published in 1812, is the kind of exception that has placed his book high on collectors' desiderata. Based probably on a slight sketch of the artist, the printmakers have transformed it into a harmony of ink tones and colors, the looped nets receding in a diminuendo, the larger sections at the bankside, diaphanous enough to allow a misty view of the distant shoreline, gradually diminishing in size and transparency as they stretch along supporting poles into the bay. Summarily denoted sails mark distant boats and, almost beyond eyesight, is the faintest shape of a far-off headland, with no more than a suggestion of pink in the sky above. It is impossible to believe that the drawing submitted by Koshū could have had explicit instruction to the block maker and color printer: it is to them finally that the print owes its gentle strength.

34

PLATE 34
NISHIMURA NANTEI (1775–1834)
Festival Procession
From *Nantei gafu kohen*
楠亭画譜後篇
(*Nantei's Drawing Album*). Second series
1826

There is a mistaken notion that only Edo-based Ukiyo-e artists depicted the daily passing show, and it is true that they were primarily concerned with the so-called Floating World. But artists of the classical school located in and around Kyoto, especially those of the Shijō following, also drew their material from the everyday life of the people, and Soken, Nangaku, Suiseki, Chinnen, and Nantei, among many others, produced books that consist of pictures of this kind. As a nation, the Japanese have always enjoyed the life around them, in street or countryside, and indeed, for most people these arenas of activity, of comings and goings, provided endless interest to lives that were by and large humdrum. Nantei was responsible for two books, the first printed in *sumi* in 1804, the sequel in color, published in 1826, which pullulate with life captured in the city or its countrified environs. He had a vivacious line, almost excessively wild in the first series, but agreeably slowed down in the sequel, as if the need to accommodate color had to some extent tempered the exuberance of the brush line.

Festival processions were a frequent distraction in the streets of Kyoto, and Nantei has given a lively impression of a segment of the crowd, the half-visible float drawing in its wake a random band of followers, the limpid color spaced in such a way as to harness the composition and its driving motion.

PLATE 35
KAWAMURA BUMPŌ (1779–1821)
Peasant Dwellings Seen Through Trees
From *Bumpō gafu*
鳳画譜 I
(*A Book of Drawings by Bumpō*). First series
1807

Bumpō seems to sum up all the finer qualities of the cultured world of Kyoto. Judging by his paintings and the many books of his prints, he was a true son of the City of Peace, and no one has given a more intimate tribute to its physical aspect than Bumpō in his four-volume topography *Teito gakei ichiran, Choice Sights of the Capital* (1809–16). He owes the idiosyncracy of his brush style to his initial study under Kishi Ganku, a pronounced mannerist, but in other respects he is wholly Shijō, in his verve, his humanity, his poetry, his clubbability.

An earlier book, dating from 1803, presented miniature staffage figures drawn from Chinese sources, but by 1807 he had convinced the publishers that he had the common touch to intrigue a wide public, and the first *gafu* was produced, an album of varied studies that must have been immediately popular in Japan, since two further series were issued in 1811 and 1813. Once known in the West, they have never ceased to charm and astonish.

Nothing could be simpler in subject than the glimpse of two small dwellings behind a fortification of bare trees. They are on a slope and approached by a flight of uneven steps which a peasant is descending, and there is a distant range of hills faintly indicated in blue. Summary dabs of pink on the cottage walls complete the sparse coloring. Bumpō's magic is in the placement of this commonplace scene in such a way that the cottages are vignetted in the jagged twigs, with empty, unexplained space beyond.

36

PLATE 36
KAWAMURA BUMPŌ
Private View
From ***Bumpō gafu***. Third series
鳳画譜 Ⅲ
1813

Typically, Bumpō transposes what was no doubt a fairly common Japanese scene to a Chinese locale. Gatherings of literati for the recital of verses and the exhibition of paintings, as we know from printed accounts and manuscript diaries, were frequent in Kyoto, and Bumpō, with his wide sympathies, must have been a welcome participant. The classically robed aficionados are disposed about the impromptu gallery with an instinctive feeling for spacing and display all Bumpō's virtuosity in handling draped figures with realism and a certain eccentricity that harks back to Ganku. The paintings, as befits the seriousness of connoisseurs, are all in pronounced Chinese taste: landscapes, bamboo, an auspicious bird, and a sheet of bold calligraphy.

37

PLATE 37
KAWAMURA BUMPŌ
Persimmons
From *Kimpaen gafu*
金波園画譜
(*The Drawing Book of Kimpaen*)
1820

In the *Bumpō gafu* series, Bumpō shows himself as something of an exhibitionist, with a freshness in his fluent handling of the brush that leads us to number him among the most urbane of masters. At heart, he seems to have been a conservative, and when you compare a late work like the *Persimmons* from the *Kimpaen gafu* with any of the prints in the *Suiseki gafu,* second series (Nos. 31–2), published in the same year, you are conscious that Bumpō is still harking back to the Chinese models in the *Mustard Seed Garden* that had fired an earlier generation, whereas Suiseki was exploring new territory, and even prevailing on the printmakers to forgo their habitual finesse in the cause of a more striking image. Bumpō remained an artist of immense charm and popularity, whereas Suiseki has to be seen as a nonconformist of genius.

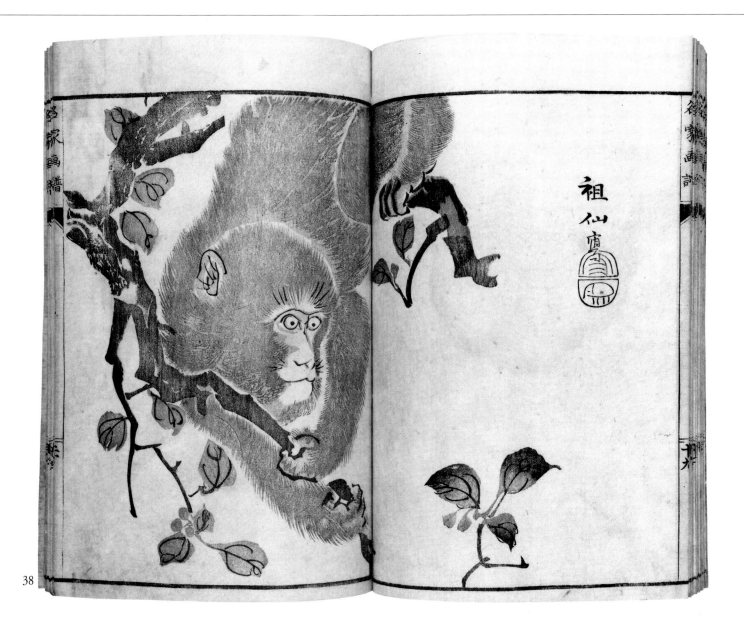

PLATE 38
MORI SOSEN (1747–1821)
Monkey
From *Meika gafu*
名家画譜
(*A Book of Paintings by Celebrated Artists*)
1814

Animals abound in Japanese paintings and prints of all schools, but most frequently they attracted artists stemming from Ōkyo and Goshun and especially the masters of the Mori subschool. Not all the greatest artists are adequately represented in book or album in printed form, and this would have been true of Mori Sosen, noted above all as a painter of monkeys, had he not been swept into the net of one of the foremost anthologies, *Meika gafu*, to which he was persuaded

to contribute the magnificent *Monkey*. No one ever equaled Sosen in his portrayal of not only the externals of this animal, the lithe suppleness of its movements, its lustrous fur, but also the very nature of the beast, its intense concentration on the object of its immediate interest (the *Meika gafu* print is typical), its reaction to its surroundings and to companions.

Meika gafu has already been referred to as one of the finest anthologies, of prime importance to anyone intent on forming a representative collection of Japanese books with prints. It was normal for artists and calligraphers to associate in joint enterprises of this kind, and harmony was furthered by the fact that pictures and inscriptions alike were cut on woodblocks.

Sosen's print bears only his signature and seal, but the block cutter has given a rich texture to the print by the distinction he has drawn between the monkey's fur and the branch to which it clings.

MORI SHUNKEI (active early 19th century)
Insects on Reeds and *Waterside Plants and Lotus*
From *Shunkei gafu*
春渓画譜
(*The Drawing Book of Shunkei*)
1820

The year 1820 was something of an *annus mirabilis* in regard to the publication of books of *kachō-e*, that is, flowers, birds, and other living creatures. R. had not thought to specialize in this field, but just by a process of acquiring any book of outstanding beauty that came his way, had brought together the *Suiseki gafu*, second series (Nos. 31–2), the Bumpō *Kimpaen gafu* (No. 37), and the *Shunkei gafu*, all 1820 publications. The Suiseki and the Bumpō have already been contrasted, and the Shunkei differs from both not merely because the artist is hybridizing two styles of painting, that of Utamaro as expressed in his great *Mushi erabi* (*Selected Insects*), of 1788, and that of the Mori subschool of animal painters, but because the publishers chose to have them printed with a meticulous precision also with some deference to *Mushi erabi*, even to the extent of adding mica here and there to highlight diaphanous wings of insects or the sheen of reptiles' bodies.

Shunkei was a pupil of Sosen (No. 38) and followed the rest of the Mori family in dedicating his paintings and a few books to plants (especially the *asagao*, morning glory), birds, and insects. No. 39 is a design that must owe its inspiration to one of the *Insect Book* prints of Utamaro. No. 40, on the other hand, is more classical Chinese in origin and reverberates with much that lies at the heart of Oriental religion and philosophy.

39

40

41

PLATE 41
KABOCHA SŌEN (active 1830s)
Waning Flower Viewing
From *Ryūkō meibutsu shi*
柳巷名物誌
(*Noted Products of Willow Street*)
1834

This book is an anthology of *kyōka,* that species of "crazy verse" peculiar to Japan, conceived as skits on the classical *waka* poems, irrational, jokey, scurrilous, and considered low class, though much enjoyed by the *haut ton.* From the late 18th century they were extremely popular, for several decades publications were frequent, and artists were often asked to provide pictorial accompaniment, though rarely actual illustration in the true sense of the word. They have figured little so far in this selection from R.'s books since they belong more appositely to the Ukiyo-e books dealt with later, but Sōen, more in the Shijō circle than the Ukiyo-e (judging by his style, for nothing is known about him), crosses the boundary and comes fittingly between earlier artists and Chinnen and Soshin.

Besides, the print chosen illustrates perfectly the whimsy of the *kyōka* addict with his habit of mocking the classical and academic. Not that Sōen in his print is following a theme provided by an actual *kyōka,* concerned as they are with customs and noted articles produced in the Yoshiwara area: rather, he is portraying a theme that might well have been the foundation of a *kyōka.* It makes fun of the *hanami,* the flower-viewing ceremony sacred to all right-thinking Japanese. It is entitled *Waning* [or *Balding*] *Flower Viewing* — the flowering trees being protected with blue parasols, which form the surprising, not to say ludicrous, decorative element to a spring landscape, and give a punning allusion to the "balding" trees.

42

PLATE 42
ŌNISHI CHINNEN (1792–1851)
Fuji Seen Through a Grove of Pine Trees
From *Sonan gafu*
楚南画譜
(*A Book of Drawings by Sonan*)
1834

As an outcome of the study I made of the Shijō school for my book called *The Uninhibited Brush,* I came to regard Ōnishi Chinnen and Suzuki Nanrei as the ultimate masters, paradigms who brought the essentials of the style to their unique consummation. Nanrei, though a prolific sketcher and at his best in the album format, was never given a retrospective *gafu* where his flamboyant gifts could be widely exploited, and, in woodcut form, he is known only by a few impres-

sive *surimono* and contributions to anthologies. Chinnen, on the other hand, also a major contributor to *gassoku,* "joint works," was taken up by the picture-book publishers and designed several books that rank among the finest produced in 19th-century Japan. The most outstanding and the most expressive of Chinnen's particular genius is *Sonan gafu* (Sonan being one of his art names).

Of the many remarkable prints in this *gafu, Fuji Seen Through a Grove of Pine Trees* has always been admired. A common enough motif, it is given surprising *éclat* by the dramatic simplification of the pines, seemingly thrown on to the paper with an urgency, as if to capture Fuji before it fades into the enveloping atmosphere. The best of Shijō often has this sense of a compelling need of the artist to capture a breathtaking but fleeting moment of beauty or strangeness that otherwise would be lost.

43

Plate 43
ŌNISHI CHINNEN
Koto Player
From *Sonan gafu*
楚南画譜
1834

What makes this print so winning to us? The line is unerring, direct and expressive: the set of the head, the evocativeness of the unfinished cheekline, the elaborate hairdo reduced to a contorted blob, the slant of the hand, drawn back in the conventional position to indicate polite submissiveness, the summary outline of the instrument placed firmly on the floor and forming a satisfying counterpoint to the figure. Once it is analyzed, one can itemize the felicities of this drawing, which the printmakers have enhanced with a discreet underscoring of color: but the sum total is a joint achievement of the artist and the man, or men, who transformed it into a masterly print.

44

PLATE 44
TANI BUNCHŌ (1763–1840) and **ŌNISHI CHINNEN**
Butterfly and Eggplant
From *Aratama chō*
新玉帖
(*Album of the New Year*)
c. 1829

Shijō artists (and, more rarely, artists of other schools) occasionally felt impelled to join forces. At some times, either two or more would collaborate on a single entity on one sheet; at other times, the individual units would remain separate though linked, as, to take a typical example, a joint grouping of the twelve zodiacal animals on a single scroll. Often, as in this joint sketch of a butterfly and eggplant,

there is no obvious reason why two artists should have come together to put two trifles together and produce — another trifle! Either was quite capable of handling it alone.

Tani Bunchō had a penchant for sketching butterflies and it may have been an act of homage on Chinnen's part to share a page with the renowned and revered master. But who can tell at this distance in time? How, indeed, were these occasional volumes of verse and print put together? The genesis of an album such as this must have been the desire of a group of *kyōka* scribblers to get into print — one of the prefaces is by Yomo Utagaki Magao, indefatigable in promoting this species of verse; the remaining prints are by Ukiyo-e, Kanō, and Independent artists, with totally unconnected thematic material. There is no norm for this type of book: each is full of the unexpected, and therein lies part of its attraction.

45

Plate 45
Maruyama Ōritsu (1817–1875)
Kamigami
From *Tama hiroi*
たまひろい
(*A Gathering of Jewels*)
1861

The downhill trend of Shijō, sensed in the *Yomo no umi,* is patent for all to see in the anthology *Tama hiroi,* published in 1861. If the untitled album of 1793 (see Nos. 23–24) may be looked on as the first manifesto of those introducing Shijō in graphic form, the *Tama hiroi* represents a *Who's Who* of those still practicing the style in 1861, and indeed, between the years 1793 and 1861, most of the finest Shijō books were published. But it has to be said that here and there the printmakers managed to give an impression of a virile art form, producing a few prints, with minimal color, that belie the notion of an art in decline. In fact, the translation into woodcuts imposed a restraint that was lacking in the same artists' paintings, which tended to pursue the novel or the trivial in less controlled line and in heady color. Ōritsu was firmly in the tradition of Ōkyo (he was a pupil of Ōshin, a leading pupil of the great master) and his print of Kamigami shows a return to a conservative Chinese style that reminds us of drawings made by Ōkyo in his immaturity. Ōkyo (1733–1795), notable for his "return to nature," was to some extent responsible for the development of the Shijō style.

Plate 46
Yamagata Soshin (1818–1862)
Banner and Wheels of a Norimon
From *Kanjaku tsuizen hanashidori*
習雀追善はなしどり
(*The Liberated Birds: A Memorial Book for Kanjaku*)
1852

It happens in the West as well as the East that certain great artists are insignificantly represented in book form or not at all, or that their finest printed works are beyond the reach of the present-day collector. In such instances, sometimes the work of a pupil makes a worthwhile substitute, and in R.'s case, lacking works truly representative of Shibata Zeshin, one of the greatest 19th-century painters and lacquer artists, he has been happy to acquire books with prints by Yamagata Soshin, who, on the basis of the makeup of his name, and, more, on the basis of his style, is assumed to have been a pupil of Zeshin.

Soshin shows exactly the same flair for giving a piquancy to any theme, however prosaic, and one book gave him a wealth of opportunities, the anthology of verse and pictures published as a memorial to the immensely popular actor Nakamura Utaemon IV, who died in 1852. This sophisticated blend of color print, ink print, and literary effusion bespeaks the culture of the Kabuki fans, and the title *Kanjaku tsuizen hanashidori* is fittingly allusive for it harps upon the name Kanjaku (literally "playing with sparrows," Utaemon's nom-de-plume), with a poetic reference to the custom of freeing caged birds at funeral services. Prominent Ukiyo-e artists designed theatrical color prints for the book, and Soshin contributed an accompaniment of offhand *haiga*-like drawings, of which this is typical. The ceremonial carriage and the processional banner so unconventionally deposited on the page are enough to recall Utaemon's portrayal of noblemen of the chivalric periods and all the splendor of a *daimyō's* procession.

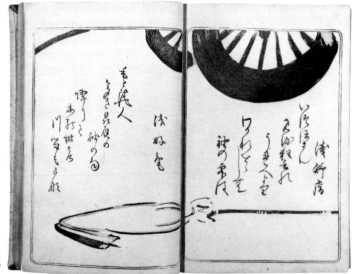

46

47

PLATE 47
YAMAGATA SOSHIN
Evening Cooling Off on the River
From *Yomo no umi*
四方海
(*Everywhere the Sea*)
c. 1857

An evening relaxation on the river, a cooling off preparatory to an elaborate meal and other, more clandestine, pleasures. The album of five rather grandiose prints, of which this is one, is known in a Japanese-owned copy with an 1857 date, and by that time, the fine flowering of the Shijō school was tending to wane, though paradoxically, the paintings tended to become more flamboyant, even aggressively so. The prints of *Yomo no umi* are relaxed and sumptuous, rather over-large, and with a hint of the vulgarization that was taking place in the taste and pursuits of the townspeople.

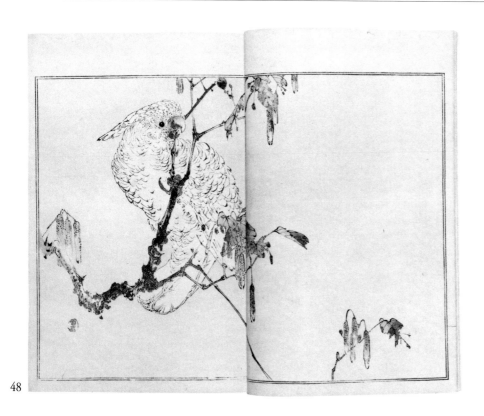

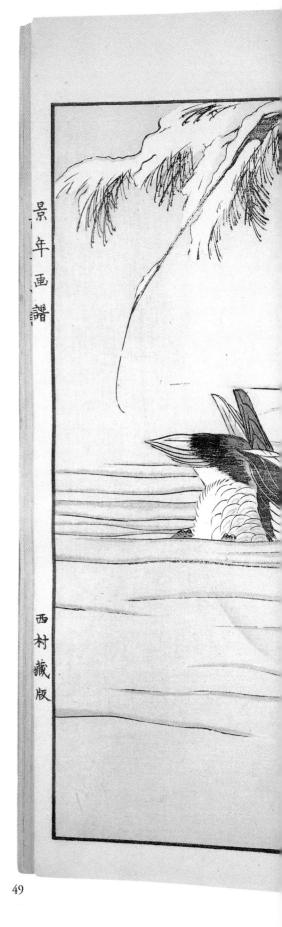

景年画譜

西村蔵版

PLATE 48
WATANABE SEITEI (1851–1918)
Parrot on a Birch Tree
From *Seitei kachō gafu*
省亭花鳥画譜
(*Seitei's Drawing Book of Flowers and Birds*), vol. 1
1890

I had intended to defer moving into the "post-Westernism" era until later, but having brought the story of Shijō so far, it would be an unwarranted disruption not to continue the evolution of bird and flower pictures so closely identified with that school. Artists like Bairei and Seitei were trained under artists who had come to maturity before Westernism had intervened, Seitei under Kikuchi Yōsai (1788–1878), who is one of the earliest to be classified as a "Japanese style" artist, a term that in reality denied a predominant mold of any school and signifies a school-less eclectic; and Bairei under two Shijō masters, Raishō and Bunrin.

The medium of both Seitei and Bairei remains the woodblock color print, but a first encounter with their book prints is decisive: they are of a different order entirely from all we have understood by Shijō or Nanga. First, as to the drawing (as in Seitei's *Parrot*), it is limned with fine lines that disown the supple brush but adequately represent the bird; second, the special qualities of the woodblock are ignored—the firm line, the blocked color, everything that made the woodcuts inimitably graphic in their own right, not mere reproductions of skillful drawings. One cannot deny that Seitei, Bairei, or Keinen give us pleasure: but it is no longer the pleasure of a graphic art where artist and printmaker fused their skills.

50

PLATE 49
IMAO KEINEN (1845–1924)
Ducks Beneath Snow-Covered Reeds
From ***Keinen kachō gafu***
景年花鳥画譜
(*Keinen's Drawing Book of Flowers and Birds*)
1891–2

Apart from the changes in technique described under No. 48, there was a move in the Meiji period to provide greatly enlarged picture books of birds and flowers, as though there was a deliberate aim to emulate the major Western albums of natural history, such as those by Redouté, Gould, Lear, Audubon, and others, copies of which had no doubt reached Japan. The printmakers manfully translated the now virtually Westernized drawings into color prints which force our admiration, though they belong to a hybrid class lacking the unique virtues of the earlier masterpieces.

PLATE 50
KŌNO BAIREI (1844–1893)
Ise Ducks
From ***Bairei hyaku-chō gafu***
媒嶺百鳥画譜
(*Bairei's Drawing Book of One Hundred Birds*)
1881

Bairei had the benefit of a sound Shijō upbringing, and his earliest drawings show he might well have become a leading Shijō painter and perhaps revitalized the moribund school. But it was impossible for any artist to escape the prevailing trend towards Westernism, and, even perhaps unwittingly (for he was active in art teaching on nationalistic lines), he succumbed. His many books of birds show him at least retaining vestiges of Shijō style, as in this print of Ise ducks and withered lotus plants.

PLATE 51
KŌNO BAIREI
Varieties of Chrysanthemum
From ***Bairei kikuhyaku shū***
媒嶺菊百種
(***Bairei's Collection of One Hundred Chrysanthemums***)
1891–6

Cultivation of varieties of this plant in Japan is something we can measure from comparison with Western indulgence in similar specialization. No one can deny the beauty of Bairei's drawing in this splendid series of albums. We may sigh for the innocent simplicity of, say, Yasukuni's *Wild Flowers* (Nos. 56–57), but it would be churlish not to admit that a book like this has to be appraised on a different level and demands respect.

53

PLATE 52
AZUMA TŌYŌ (1755–1839)
Deer in the Snow
From *Keijō gaen*
京城画苑
(*An Album of Pictures by Kyoto Artists*)
1814

Occasionally, an anthology might be given a regional basis, like *Keijō gaen*, literally *A Garden of Kyoto Paintings*. Shijō's close association with the capital is signified by Goshun appearing at the head of the procession of artists, most of whom are followers of the Shijō persuasion if not actually pupils of Goshun. Tōyō actually began his painting career under a minor Kanō practitioner in Edo, from whom he went on to further study with Taiga, Ōkyo, and Goshun. He relied on a strong, masculine brush line and forceful, rather than fanciful, composition.

The printmakers made an economical use of the medium in producing *Deer in the Snow*, and the low-key palette and the bold outline led to a curiously affecting picture, the contrast of the timid animal and the stark drift of snow suggesting a sentimentality not normally found in Tōyō's work.

One picture from an album like this can give no notion of the total artistic effect of the book held in the hand and leafed through, presenting a succession of deliciously color-printed versions of paintings by many of the principal artists whose style stems from Goshun. It is one thing to view a single sheet lifted from an album or a book, but it should be remembered that it forms only a contributory fragment to a much greater whole.

54

PLATE 53
KATSUMA RYŪSUI (1711–1796)
Stag and Hind
From *Wakana*
わかな
(*Fresh Shoots*)
1756

I have already stressed that anthologies of verse and print comprise a number of uniquely beautiful books of Japan, and here by way of interlude a few can be sampled before we shift to different schools of painters. The anthologies quite often embrace the work of artists of differing styles. One of the most notable, partly because of the extensive use of color printing at the early date of 1756, is called, quite simply, *Wakana* (*Fresh Shoots*). It is one of those limited-edition books called *kubari-hon*, private publications, compiled in this case by a coterie of haiku poets to commemorate the 17th anniversary of the death of Doppo-an Chōha (1703–1740), whom they revered as their teacher. Two artists supplied the prints to accompany Chōha's poems, Hanabusa Ippō, pupil of the renegade Kanō artist Hanabusa Itchō, and Katsuma Ryūsui, also of Itchō's circle, but in style still further away from Kanō orthodoxy. Ippō's prints are in *sumi*, but Ryūsui, who is known almost entirely by his book prints, relied on color printing, as he did in two other notable books, *Boon of the Sea* (1762) and *Boon of the Mountains* (1763).

The best known of the color prints in *Wakana* is one of two women in Heian dress, which seems to anticipate the richness of the *nishiki-e*, or "brocade prints," designed by Harunobu from 1764 onwards, but I have chosen the *Stag and Hind*, no less enchanting and of a decorative order that recalls Kōrin.

PLATE 54
MATSUMOTO HŌJI (dates not known)
Toad
From *Meika gafu*
名家画譜
(*A Book of Paintings by Celebrated Artists*)
1814

This truly great anthology has already been introduced under No. 38 (Mori Sosen). The publishers indulged in blatant hyperbole in the title of the book, for the term "celebrated" certainly cannot be applied to all the artists featured. Hōji, in fact, is almost unknown apart from this fatuous toad, and Mitchell, in his never-to-be-over-praised *Biobibliography*, added the note "Studied paintings under Buson. Especially skillful at drawing frogs." There is no doubt about the mesmeric force of the blank eyes of this toad (there is always doubt in the lay mind about the distinction between toad and frog). Immensely enlarged, the print proved a highly successful attraction when it was used as a poster for the exhibition of my Japanese books at the British Museum in 1980.

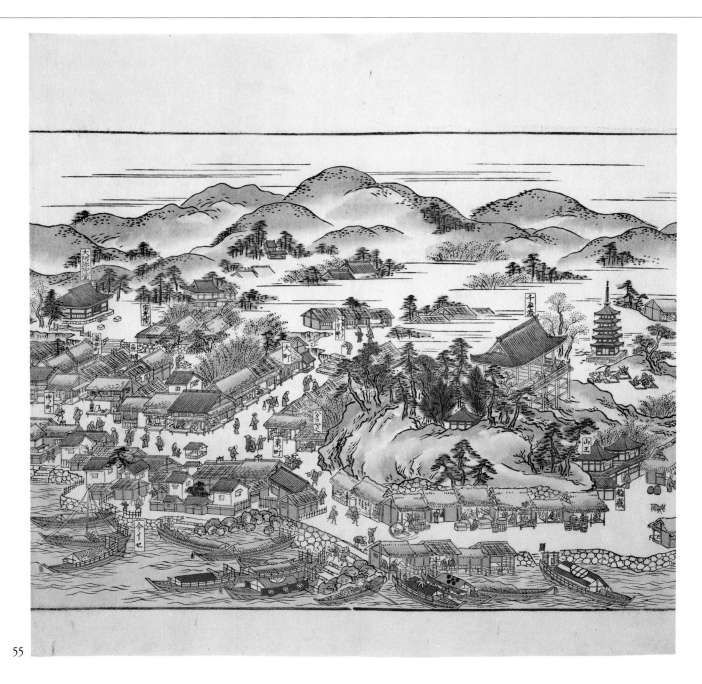

55

Plate 55
Tachibana Morikuni (1679–1748)
Harbor
From *Aki no kuni Itsukushima shōkei*
安芸国厳島勝景
(*Fine Views of Itsukushima in Aki Province*)
1720

Only a small proportion of prints after Kanō artists figure in the makeup of this book. As the upholders of orthodoxy and academism, a great deal of their many illustrated books are worthy, but dull, without impact on the collector like R., searching for qualities that intrigue and provoke surprise and admiration. But by the time his collection had encompassed the Nanga and Shijō works so far dis-

cussed he felt the urge to widen his horizon and to learn to appreciate Japanese art of all denominations. In this way, a few examples of Kanō art had been acquired.

Morikuni was a stalwart Kanō artist but his *meisho-ki* (quite factual topography) would not normally have caught R.'s eye. However, he was immediately drawn to the Itsukushima volumes by reason of the delightful, jewellike hand-coloring of the set which came his way. Without color, the designs are prosaic enough, but the colorist has breathed life into them, and it has been suggested that it may have been Morikuni himself who embellished them. It cannot be ruled out that this was a set specially commissioned by some noble client, but, more likely, the painting was the work of some proud owner who responded to the challenge of the unadorned outlines.

56

PLATES 56–57
TACHIBANA YASUKUNI (1717–1792)
Marsh Marigolds and Irises and *Poppies and Bijin-sō*
From *Ehon noyamagusa*
絵本野山草
(*A Picture Book of Wild Flowers*)
1754

At the date this book was published, color printing was something rare and costly, and however desirable for a botanical work, it was quite ruled out for a five-volume herbal like *Ehon noyamagusa*. But the block cutters showed immense resource and, denied color, they used their skills to simulate a range of tone and texture. The treatment of the poppy heads demonstrates the effective contrast where some petals are picked out in white reserve on black and others where the petals are simply in black line. The result is a suggestion of different coloring. The handling of the leaves is also distinctive: the differing tones of the upper and lower surfaces are emphasized by a similar variation in conveying the veining, and the strong writhing lines on the darker side give flexibility and a sense of motion to the foliage. In the other example from this book, a strong pattern and *mise-en-page* is set up by the alternation of the dark masses of flowers and some leaves and the firm outlines of the blades of the irises and the lower parts of the marsh marigold plants.

This was not a serious botanical work, and though it presents accurate drawings, they are simply labeled with their popular names, and there are no details of structure or habitat. But it was surprisingly popular and was republished a number of times, the latest in 1883 when color blocks, advertised as designed by Hasegawa Sadanobu, were added to the original line blocks cut for the first, 1754, edition.

57

PLATE 58
KAWANABE KYŌSAI (1831–1889)
Bats and Momiji
From *Kyōsai rakuga*
暁斎楽画
(*Kyōsai's Drawings for Pleasure*)
1881

Kyōsai's *Rakuga* represents a leap of over a century forward, but Kyōsai is essentially a Kanō artist, even if he departed from the strict canons of the school inculcated by his early master Tōhaku and had instruction from the Ukiyo-e artist Kuniyoshi. Never merely conformist, he developed an independence that is more noticeable in his work in book form than in his more serious paintings, which continued to reflect his Kanō upbringing.

Rakuga is typical of Kyōsai in his racy, rumbustious vein, wholly extrovert and eccentric. The *Bats* is a vivacious drawing, and the scattered *momiji* leaves, almost the only notes of color, help to further the centrifugal confusion of the design.

58

59

60

HISHIKAWA MORONOBU (c. 1618–1694)
The Evening Cup of Sake and *Parting at Dawn*
From *Koi no mutsugoto: shijū hatte*
恋の睦言四十八手
(*Whisperings of Love: Thirty-eight Situations*)
1679

It was inevitable, given R.'s searching mind and impressionability to depictions of different peoples and their life-styles, that he would be attracted eventually by Ukiyo-e, whose very name, "Pictures of the Floating World," made it plain they were concerned with the "passing show." Although the life of the commoner had crept into the background of the early Yamato-e scrolls, devoted usually to more elevated subjects, the townsfolk and peasants took center stage in the work of certain plebeian artists in the 17th century, and Moronobu, though not the founder of the school, brought the tentative beginnings to a recognizable style and so justifies his being called its founding father. Ukiyo-e was not simply an extension of the subject matter of Japanese painting but the creation of a new style of painting, more factual and colorful than classical styles, utilizing pigments made opaque by the addition of powdered shell, *gofun,* and expanding its audience by the widespread use of woodcut illustration in book and album form.

Remembering the hedonism of the parvenu classes in Edo and Osaka, it is easy to understand the popularity of erotic painted scrolls, and soon after, of erotic prints in picture book and album. The inclusion of illustration from such works in modern surveys of Japanese art has long been a source of contention, and although the absolute veto on explicit sex pictures has been modified in recent years to permit their inclusion in books of serious intent bearing on social and artistic aspects, there are recognizable limits. The potential audience is the predetermining factor. Many people are still shocked and offended by pictures of couples making love, and if a book is intended for a nonspecialist readership, it is thought best to err on the side of prudence. That is the attitude adopted in these extracts from the collection made by R., who has been guided by artistic merit only.

The sad fact is that to avoid erotica in an artist like Moronobu, the outstanding master of Ukiyo-e in the 17th century, is to rule out some of his finest books. So, in selecting from *Koi no mutsugoto,* one of his notable early *shunga* ("spring pictures," i.e., erotica), I have chosen two of the four opening, or "cover," sheets, which are no more than romantic, at least to our eyes, not explicitly erotic, as are the ensuing prints. Neither is of a kind to give us the slightest qualm today, though in the Japan of the 17th century, the pictures and the titles were highly charged. Moronobu, in 1679, was approaching the highest peak of his achievement in the early 1680s: the figures are supple and naturalistically linked; the woodcuts contrast the rhythmic outlines with conventional patterning and achieve a lively blend, peculiar to the ink woodcut of this so-called primitive period. They represent an important stage in the development of the woodblock ink print in Japan.

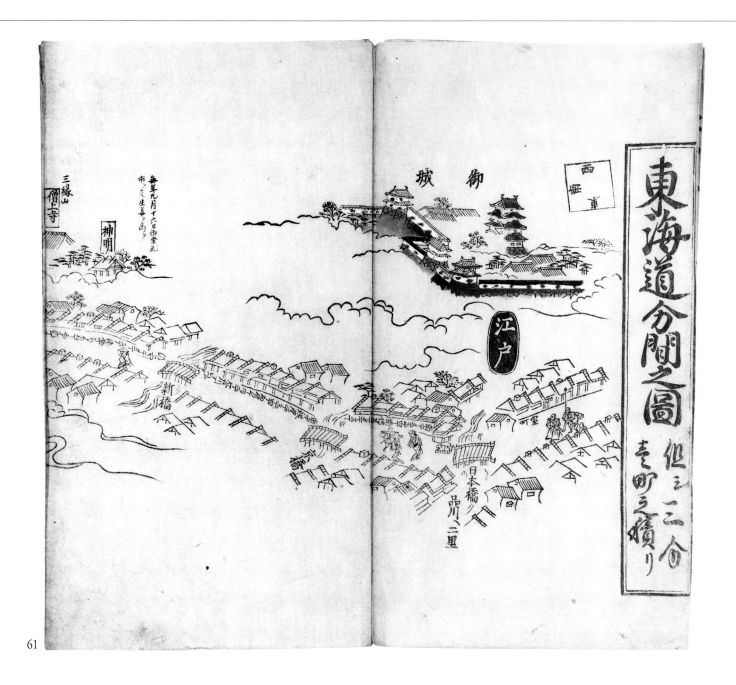

三縁山
僧□寺

神明

毎年九月十六日御奉孔
市っを生善ヶ島ヶ

新橋

御城

西
無
重

江戸

日本橋ノ
品川ニ二里

東海道分間之圖
但ヲ二合
壱町ヲ續リ

61

PLATE 61
HISHIKAWA MORONOBU
Edo, Nihon-bashi to Shinagawa
From *Tōkaidō bunken ezu*
東海道分間絵図
(*A Measured Pictorial Map of the Tōkaidō*)
1690

The Ukiyo-e artist, even one as eminent as Moronobu, was at the beck and call of publishers of many different kinds. It was valuable for publicity to attach his name even to a map with useful information for travelers, such as this of the Tōkaidō, the most famous highway in Japan, linking Edo, the seat of the Shogun, the dictator and de facto ruler, in the east, and Kyoto, the ancient capital, in the west. Moronobu worked to the drawings of Ochikochi Dōin, who was already known for an earlier map of Edo. The Tōkaidō map was to the scale of three *bu* (approximately 3/8ths of an inch) to one *chō* (about 120 yards). It is in five volumes and unfolds laterally in the hand.

There is nothing particularly distinguished about Moronobu's map, but it serves to keep in perspective the humdrum activity expected of a painter who, as an artist of the figure, was supreme. The first stage of the Tōkaidō encompassed three bridges, Nihon-bashi, Kyō-bashi, and Shin-bashi, named in this fragment showing the distance (two *ri,* about six miles) to the staging post at Shinagawa.

62

This is the third volume of a set of three with a hand-brushed title on the cover (slightly misleading, as it changes the order of the words, giving *Kimigayo nyōhitsu*). It is one of a number of books that Sukenobu designed in the early 1730s purporting to give women instruction in letter writing and providing evidence of the extremes to which calligraphy could be stretched. The eccentric calligrapher for a number of these books was the well-known Hasegawa Myōtei, and the book title in the odd volume owned by R. includes the first line of a poem in the *Manyōshū*, one of Japan's earliest anthologies, intended to give the work a suitable respectability.

But the frontispiece and sole print in R.'s volume represents a reserved, pensive young woman seated and holding in her hands a letter handed to her by a kneeling attendant. She does not strike us as being sophisticated enough to read the letter—in the same extravagant grass writing as the bewildering examples provided in the book. It is the sort of paradoxical situation posed by Ukiyo-e artists to entertain their quick-witted audience. Sukenobu saw a perverse attraction in the almost illegible scrawl and the near-abstract designs so produced, and it is doubtful that he was seriously offering instruction on how to employ it or how to decipher it.

PLATES 62–63
NISHIKAWA SUKENOBU (1671–1751)
Young Woman Receiving a Letter and
A page of free-flowing calligraphy
From *Nyōhitsu: Kimigayo*
女筆君が代
(*Women's Calligraphy in an Early Classic*)
c. 1730s

In Kyoto, in the first half of the 18th century, Sukenobu created an ideal of womanhood differing radically from Moronobu's: in stature, she is closer to the normal *musume* (maiden), frailer and gentler. In his numerous picture books, Sukenobu portrays her with lines less bold than the Edo master used, but more effeminately rounded. She is lissome and winning, and soon becomes the general favorite to whom all Ukiyo-e artists, Kyoto or Edo, succumb. She is the trendsetter who reaches her apotheosis in Harunobu's slender child-woman.

In R.'s collection, there are a number of volumes full of typical Sukenobu prints, but one selects itself by reason of its singularity.

63

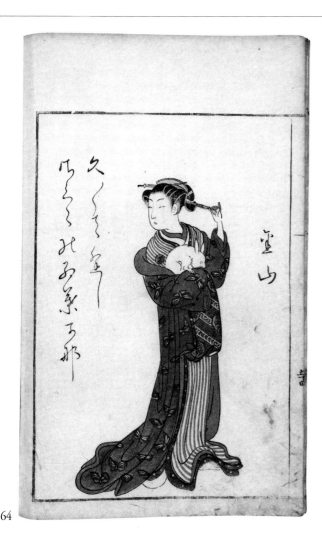

64

today, by reason of qualities that lie outside sheer artistry and have more to do with the projection of a new idea of femininity.

In the book world, Harunobu's greatest contribution is the (*Ehon*) *seirō bijin awase* of 1770, a series of full-length pictures of courtesans, in which color printing reached heights only sustained to the same degree in a work published a few months earlier, the Shunshō/Bunchō *Ehon butai ōgi* (*The Picture Book of Stage Fans*) (not in the R. Collection). In fact, R. owns only Vol. 4 of the five forming the Harunobu book, and while normally R. would resist accepting an incomplete work, in this instance, he was justified: the single volume is in fine state with relatively unimpaired color; complete copies are extremely rare; and, to be honest, a sampling of the contents is quite representative and avoids the monotony given by a complete set of the 166 color prints in the five volumes.

The book was designed in the last year or two of Harunobu's life, and a certain languor and satiety are sensed. Kameyama, standing with a white hare balanced in the crook of her right arm, is vacantly adjusting one of her hairpins; she is prinked out in a red-striped kimono under a maroon *uchikake* bearing a pattern of butterflies. Shigezuru stands half-turned to the left, her limp form the very pattern of boredom.

PLATES 64–65
SUZUKI HARUNOBU (1724–1770)
The Courtesan Kameyama Holding a White Hare
and *The Courtesan Shigezuru*
From (**Ehon**) *seirō bijin awase*
絵本青楼美人合
(*Picture Book Comparison of the Beauties
of the Green Houses*), vol. 4
1770

It is no doubt an exaggeration to imagine we can study the changes in society in Japan in the picture books of Moronobu, Sukenobu, and Harunobu, since to a large extent they present only the queens of the licensed quarters and the women of the lower orders. They do, however, record the vogue among the literate commoners for this or that type of woman and her apparel and so act as a barometer of taste in general among them. Harunobu had the advantage of color printing of exquisite subtlety and this, coupled with the etherealized forms of the girls, the seemingly infantine innocence of their demeanor, even when, as so often, they were prostitutes, led to prints that hold sway even

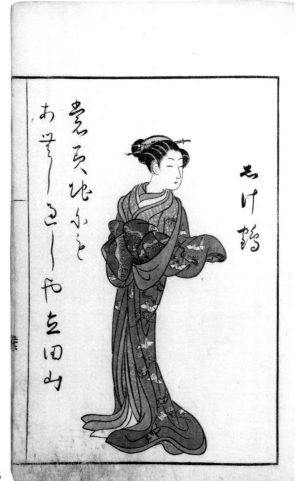

65

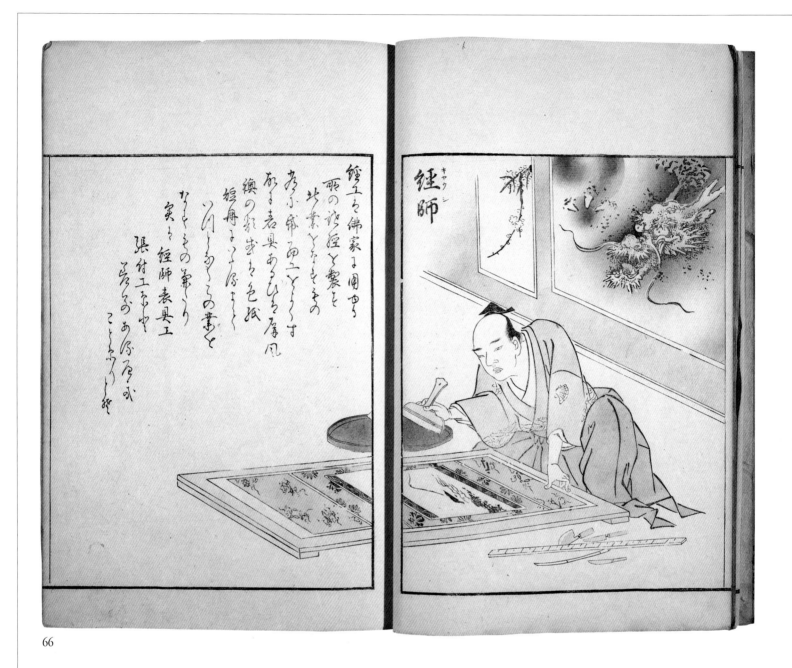

PLATE 66
TACHIBANA MINKŌ (active mid-18th century)
Kakemono Mounter
From *Saiga shokunin burui*
彩画職人部類
(*Various Classes of Artisan in Colored Pictures*)
1771

The most remarkable thing about this book is that, although the outlines are cut on the woodblock, the colors are applied by stencils (pictures so produced were called *kappazuri-e*). Stenciling was a process occasionally adopted for adding color to woodblock prints, sometimes for cheapness, as in coarse warrior or theatrical ephemera,

and occasionally in superior publications where the finesse of the stenciler gave rise to effects of inconceivable delicacy.

There was always a curiosity in Japan about the work of craftsmen, and in painting and printed form there are innumerable depictions of them from earliest times. There was an aura of respect and even mystery about certain types, especially those either considered on a par with artists, or else closely associated with one or another of the arts, and Minkō included several of these revered virtuosi — the mirror polisher, the armorer, the sword-guard maker, the mask maker, the potter, and the *kakemono* mounter, depicted here.

This book is Minkō's major work. He is known otherwise by a small number of *surimono* and *surimono*-like prints, produced around the 1765 date, and by a few minor books.

PLATE 67
KITAO MASANOBU (1761–1816)
The Poet Tsuburi no Hikaru
From *Temmei shinsen gojūnin isshu:
Azuma-buri kyōka bunko*
天明新鐫五十人一首吾妻曲狂文庫
*(Newly Block-Cut in Temmei: A Poem of Each of Fifty
Poets: A Bookcase of Edo Kyōka)*
1786

The crazy verse, *kyōka*, has been touched on earlier. In Temmei, the period from 1780 to 1789, it was all the rage, and this book, with its unwieldy title, is one of two that Masanobu dedicated to the leading writers of such verse. The first, published in 1786, was confined to contemporary exponents, the other, a year later, extended to one hundred poets of past and present.

Masanobu, equally successful as an author of light literature and as a painter and book illustrator, was the ideal artist for books of this kind. He was witty and irreverent and had more than his share of the streak of irrationality that runs through the nature of the Japanese male at all times. The *kyōka* was a skit on the classical *waka* verse: Masanobu carries the joke further by classifying his selections into fifty or one hundred, in imitation of the groupings of the "immortal" Fifty or One Hundred. What is more, he makes it plain that he is portraying comic poets by absurdities of dress or behavior — Saketsuki Komehi sits covering his head with a pillow; Kanerachi is walking in the snow under an umbrella that has a prominent hole in the roof, and his attendant page puts his hand to his face to hide his expression of disbelief; and Tsuburi no Hikaru rides a pantomime horse holding a fan picturing Fuji, and so distantly evoking a famous classical scene of the poet Narihira, traveling east.

67

PLATES 68–69
KITAGAWA UTAMARO (1754–1806)
Pheasants and Wagtail and *Wren and Snipe*
From *Momo chidori kyōka awase*
百千鳥狂歌合
(Birds Compared in Humorous Verses)
c. 1791

Too often Utamaro has been judged exclusively on his color prints of the social scene in Edo and especially his superb pictures of beautiful women, but he also designed many masterful books and albums which justify his placement among the highest elite of the Ukiyo-e artists. The books form three main groups: those devoted to the natural world — flowers, insects, birds, shells; those that are in the nature of annuals with a variety of scenes, either contemporary or evocative of the past; and *shunga*. The albums of *Birds* and *Shells* had been announced in the *Insect Book* of 1788 (not in the R. Collection). They were intended to accompany *kyōka*, but, unlike the verses, the prints are quite serious works of art on which Utamaro staked his reputation. The publisher was Tsutaya Jūsaburō, the most renowned of this or any other period; the color printing was of a high standard, and every one of the albums is remarkable for truly great graphic art.

Throughout the two volumes of the *Birds* book, Utamaro not only contrives to give lively portrayals of various species, but composes elegant arrangements of them in their natural habitats. The pair of pheasants and a wagtail form an imposing pyramidal group, with verses balanced at either side. The Japanese wren sings from a hanging branch that provides a foil at one corner to the springing reeds giving cover to the pair of snipe at lower left. The calligraphy of the verses is neatly placed above the snipe, leaving free play to the looping twigs of the branch.

73

68

69

74

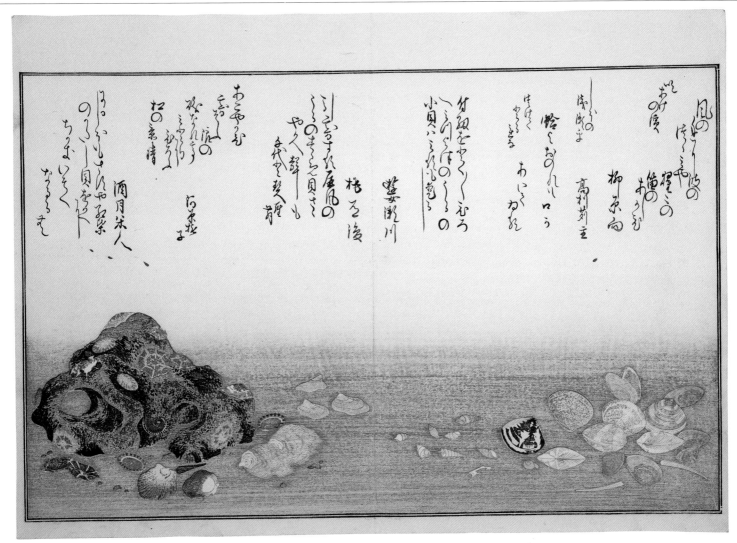

70

KITAGAWA UTAMARO
Shells On and Around a Conical Rock
and *The Shell Game*
From *Shioi no tsuto*
潮干のつと
(*Treasures of the Ebb Tide*)
c. 1790

However beautiful the single pages reproduced from this book, they can never adequately convey the ultimate appeal of the complete album when viewed as a whole, held in the hand and presenting the total effect aimed at by the book designer in collaboration with artist, block cutter, and printer. Of all Utamaro's albums this factor is most evident in the shell book, which was planned, within hand-painted covers, as a work of conscious book-making art, with poems, preface, and other text pages interleaved with eight exquisite color prints, an introductory view of shell gatherers at Shinagawa Bay, six sheets of arrangements of diverse shells and sea-wrack, and a final scene of girls playing the shell game in an elegant room.

The color printmakers rose to the challenge, and each group of shells demanded technical accomplishment of the highest order, deploying embossing and the application of mica and metal dusts to produce the sparkle and sheen of surfaces varying from shell to shell. This was in no sense a book of conchology: the shells so attractively displayed are in no logical order and serve as an embellishment to quantities of flippant and suggestive *kyōka*. The two scenes that introduce and conclude the pages of shells are among the most appealing of Utamaro's album prints. The gathering of the shells is the occasion for a plein-air scene of serene atmosphere; the girls playing with the shells evoke an intimate gathering in a room open to the garden.

72

PLATE 72

KITAGAWA UTAMARO
Moonlight on the Yoshiwara
From *Ehon kyōgetsubō*
絵本狂月坊
(*Picture Book of the Mad Full Moon*)
1789

Ehon kyōgetsubō is one of those annuals published by Tsutaya that gave series of pictures of legendary or traditional subjects alongside contemporaneous ones, always with *kyōka* verses. The title was no doubt intended to be obscure and the translation given is one of a number that have been proposed. In addition to the print illustrated here, the scenes are of Yukihira, a medieval poet of imperial descent on the beach at Suma, where he had been banished; a woodman crossing a bridge over a torrent, surprisingly in Kanō style in tones of *sumi;* peasants near their cottage; the Emperor Gensō, crossing the fabled aerial bridge towards the Palace of the Moon. In each print, the leitmotiv is the full moon.

Only the print illustrated is strictly Ukiyo-e in style, with the location identified by the embankment leading up to the licensed quarters; the other prints suggest Kanō, Itchō, Tosa, and even Chinese styles, and this half-playful eclecticism was a curious feature of several of Tsutaya's annuals.

PLATES 73–74

KITAGAWA UTAMARO
Shadows on the Shōji and *Snow Scene:*
Barge Towed along a River
From *Gin sekai*
銀世界
(*The Silver World*)
1790

The Silver World is another of Tsutaya's *kyōka* albums, five color prints devoted to the theme of snow, with a wide range of locale and style. The picture of an interior shows a geisha leaving a convivial gathering, a maidservant seeing her out and revealing the falling snow as she slides back the door. Behind a screen sheltering the guests from the draft, the party continues in full swing, and the artifice of showing shadowy forms of the participants through the transparent *shōji* is a masterstroke of artist and printmaker. The subtlety of the printing gives an illusionistic effect of forms and movement, and the monochrome of the shadows gives a heightened reality to the two figures in full color beyond the screen.

How far the printmakers heeded an artist's behests, what form their collaboration took, are still matters of debate, but in a print such as that of men towing a barge, one feels that the artist must have had some influence on how the block cutter interpreted the preliminary drawing. In this snowy landscape, the sparseness of the lines and forms means that the spaces really determine the composition, and the predominance of blank paper not only conveys the snow, but the coolness of the air. This print, again, goes beyond normal Ukiyo-e style and shows how well Utamaro could make use of understatement.

73

74

75

Plate 75
Chōbunsai Eishi (1756–1829)
Poetess and Her Poem
From *Nishi-zuri onna sanjū-rokkasen*
錦摺女三十六歌僊
(*The Thirty-six Immortal Poetesses in Brocade Prints*)
1801

Because Eishi was of samurai class, it was to be anticipated that his paintings and prints might show a greater degree of refinement than other artists', and in general it is borne out by a large proportion of his work. He was not greatly involved in designs for books, but the one named above is exceptional in just those qualities one might describe as "aristocratic." It is a series of color prints of young women calligraphers "not over fifteen years of age, pupils of the Edo master Hanagata Shōdo" and Eishi has depicted them in the finery of the Heian age and in the flamboyant hairdos of the period.

Each poetess occupies the left-hand page, and at the right is her name, and her poem in showy calligraphy. It is eminently a deluxe album.

For no logical reason that can be imagined, Hokusai provided a frontispiece of a *daimyō* and his retainers, a delightful print but with no apparent relevance to the theme of the album, or, for that matter, no equivalent to the surpassing technical brilliance of the portraits of the juvenile poetesses.

76

PLATE 76
CHŌBUNSAI EISHI
Oiran and Attendants
From *Otoko-dōka*
男踏歌
(*The Stamping Song of Men*)
1798

Tsutaya Jūsaburō died in 1797, but fine books and albums continued to come out under his imprint after that date. The title of this anthology of New Year's *kyōka* comes from one of the New Year observances dating back to the imperial court of old Japan. Several well-known artists designed the prints: Shigemasa, Utamaro, Hokusai, Tōrin, Ekiji, and Eishi, responsible for the one reproduced here. The *oiran,* the highest ranking courtesan, is in a room with a circular window through which is a wintry view of the embankment (the Nihon-tsuzumi) leading to the Yoshiwara. One of her attendants points excitedly to the scene outside; two others warm themselves at a charcoal brazier; a fourth is seated on one side of the *oiran,* who leans on a library trolley on which books and poem sheets are stacked.

77

78

KATSUSHIKA HOKUSAI (1760–1849)
Three prints from *Hokusai manga*
北斎漫画
(*Hokusai's Random Sketches*)

Of all Japanese illustrated books, Hokusai's *Manga* is best known, both to the Japanese and to the rest of the world. The first volume came out in 1814 and such was its popularity that by 1819 ten volumes has been published. By 1814, Hokusai had already proved himself master in every genre — as painter of beautiful women, as illustrator of novels, as designer of color prints of infinite variety, as creator of "poetic topography" in albums of *kyōka*. The *Manga* arose from his fecundity as a compulsive sketcher, as a producer of brush drawings of everything around him, men and women in every sort of activity, often with a streak of drollery and an eye to human weaknesses; animals and birds with a liveliness and an individuality entirely his own; landscapes that often achieve an expressive nobility. There is little more by way of text than a short introduction. Hokusai's *Manga* is by far the best known of a species of picture book dear to the Japanese heart: they doted on pictures of everything around them.

The *Manga* has the distinction of being among the earliest sources of the Japonisme movement in the West. Von Siebold, whose collection of Japanese books was mentioned in the introduction, actually published some lithographs after landscapes in Vol. 7 of the *Manga* in his own 1831 account of Japan, while Hokusai was still alive; and the French artist Félix Bracquemond became aware of the *Manga* in 1856 and was instrumental in spreading knowledge of it in France.

PLATE 77
Four Ways of Enjoying Oneself
From vol. 10
1819

Throughout the *Manga*, Hokusai portrays simple folk enjoying themselves. He poked fun at their foibles in a way that intrigued the majority of contemporary readers who naturally did not recognize themselves as the butt of his pleasantries.

In the quartet sharing the page, the smoker is pulling a face to express contentment as he puffs, the noodle eater is accused of "impolite gluttony," another is playing a game of "angling for *kaki* [persimmon]," and the fourth displays his acrobatism in disposing of rice balls. Hokusai has the deftness to convey all these actions convincingly, and the woodblock cutter is faithful to the racy brush line.

79

PLATE 78
Cleaning the Demon Guardian
From vol. 11
No date

PLATE 79
The Awa Rapids
From vol. 7
1817

In another picture, Hokusai zooms in on a trio who are cleaning a giant stone statue of one of the two guardians, the Ni-Ō, that bar demons from entering a temple. Here again, there is just a suspicion of the ludicrous in the manner in which the men are employing their tiny brushes to sluice the dust from sculptured hollows of the mighty leg, and attention is focused on he who has the senior task of pedicuring the holy foot.

The mood changes in this double-page print: from the foibles of mankind we are swept into the maelstrom at Awa. It is symptomatic of Hokusai's zest for experience that he encompasses both the quirks of human behavior and the sublimity of elemental forces. In this he is among the few that we account the greatest geniuses of pictorial art worldwide — how easily Hokusai's workmen stand beside Rembrandt's; and how few other than Leonardo can have created a tumult of waters as Hokusai did in a whirlpool of lines.

80

PLATES 80–81

KATSUSHIKA HOKUSAI
Fuji Above the Sea and *Storm over Fuji*
From *Fugaku hyakkei*
富嶽百景
(*One Hundred Views of Fuji*), vol. 2
1835

It is hard to choose, from Hokusai's immense oeuvre, another book as momentous as the *Manga*, but one above all cannot be omitted even from the restricted representation imposed by this brief survey: the *One Hundred Views of Fuji* published in two volumes in 1834–5 (and a third that was delayed until c. 1849). It is an amazing series of variations on the leitmotiv of the peak glorified as the most remarkable landscape feature of Japan, endlessly praised in rhyme and prose and constantly depicted in painting and print, until one has to see it as the emblem of Japan itself, an obsession that Hokusai brings home with all the power of his imagination and compositional flair. Here we reproduce two aspects of his handling of the theme: *Fuji Above the Sea,* one of the few designs in his work that approaches the sublimity of the most famous of all his color prints in the series *Thirty-Six Views of Fuji*; and *Storm over Fuji,* where a dazzling flash of lightning is marvelously caught by a virtuoso cooperation of the *sumi* printers.

Indeed, the *Hundred Views* is a technical triumph. In the first issues of the two volumes (known as the "Falcon Feather" edition from the design of the title label on the front cover), the *sumi* printing is surpassingly beautiful. A choice paper was used, the block cutting was to the highest standard, and the printers were meticulous in following every tone and gradation called for by the artist. A fine set of the "Falcon Feather" edition represents the ne plus ultra of monochrome printing.

PLATE 82

KATSUSHIKA HOKUSAI
Octopus Violating a Woman
From *Kinoe-no-komatsu*
喜能會之故真通
(meaning obscure), vol. 1
1814

Through an immense output during a career of more than seven decades, we come to recognize Hokusai as a man who experienced and expressed all that life has to offer. On the dark side, he agonized over the macabre and the horrific, and this picture, from one of his *shunga* books, is among his most terrifying images. It occasioned a famous passage in Edmond de Goncourt's book on Hokusai, published in Paris in 1896. He wrote:

> A terrible plate: on rocks green with marine plants is the naked body of a woman, swooning with gratification, *sicut cadaver,* to such a degree that one cannot tell whether she is drowned or alive, and an immense octopus, with frightening eye-pupils in the shape of black moon-segments, sucks the lower part of the body, while a small octopus battens on her mouth.

81

82

83

This frontispiece to one volume of another *shunga* book gives only a suggestion of the erotic nature of the main contents. In such prints, Hokusai took the opportunity to handle compositions frequently seen in separate-sheet prints by many other artists, Utamaro above all, but rarely attempted by him. By openly displaying a toothpick in her mouth, the lady shows she is not very well brought up.

84

Plate 84

HAMBEI SHŌKŌSAI (active late 18th–early 19th century)
Two Actors in a Scene from a Play
From *Ehon futaba aoi*
絵本二葉葵
(*The Seed-Leaves of the Hollyhock*)
1798

This play is recorded as having been performed in Osaka, but even without that signpost, it would have been immediately apparent that the artist belonged to that city. There is some quality, difficult to isolate, which marks not only the physiognomy of the individuals portrayed and the style of drawing as of Osaka origin: it distinguished them from products of Edo as clearly as the paintings and prints of Renaissance Florence differ from those of Venice. Even the technique of printmaking differed between Edo and Osaka: in Osaka, there was a harder, more meticulous block cutting and a somewhat stronger contrast of colors. These differentiations between the prints of the two great commercial centers fascinates R., and he was delighted to acquire this book because it proved them so conclusively.

Like other Osaka artists of Kabuki prints, Shōkōsai was strongly influenced by the Edo master Toyokuni, but he could not escape the regional bias towards physical types and technical standards.

85

Plate 85
Utagawa Kunisada (1786–1864)
An Actor as a Warrior with a Halberd
From *Yakusha sanjū-rokkasen*
俳優三十六花撰
(*A Selection of Thirty-six Flowers of the Theater*)
1835

Kabuki was a world apart, and in Edo and Osaka had a perfervid public following. Printed images of actors were in popular demand, and specialist publishers came into being to supply them. The standard level of prints and books that satisfied the majority of Kabuki followers tends to seem monotonous to outsiders, but there was a class who formed a more critical and fastidious section of the theater-going public, and for them were produced the splendid sheet prints and books that number among the outstanding achievements of the publishers. Usually, these superior books were color printed, but in the case of this Kunisada book, the publishers Nishimuraya and Nakamuraya decided to restrict the printing to *sumi*, but of the most complex kind (except only for an insert of three double-page landscapes by Hokkei with limited color). In the end, the actor prints are exemplary of *sumi* printing at its finest, and in technical mastery approach, in figures, the standard of the landscapes in Hokusai's *One Hundred Views of Fuji*.

86

PLATE 86
UTAGAWA KUNISADA
Lovers
From *Shiki no nagame*
色の詠
(*An Appraisal of Sensual Pleasure*)
c. 1830s

In contradistinction to the refinement of the *sumi* printing in the book last described, there are certain *shunga* that are among the most opulently, one might even say vulgarly, printed books of the first half of the 19th century. *Shiki no nagame* is one, with heady color and extravagant settings for violent love scenes. Here, the entwined figures are in a room looking on to a garden where a ginkgo tree is shedding leaves onto a stream.

PLATE 87
HASEGAWA MITSUNOBU
(active first half of 18th century)
Tadanobu's Gō Board
From *Toba-e fude byōshi*
鳥羽絵筆拍比
(*The Rhythm of the Brush in Toba-e*)
1724

Toba-e are a satiro-caricatural form of picture peculiar to Japan. They are further evidence of that streak of irrationality in the Japanese makeup referred to earlier, and germane therefore to R.'s coverage of Japanese output in book format, even though *Toba-e* lie outside what many would consider as serious art. The name needs explanation. Toba Sōjō was a priest-artist of A.D. 1053–1140 whose name has

88

87

been linked with painted scrolls of comic animal drawings; and when, in the 18th century, scat drawings of the type shown in this reproduction began to appear, they were, quite unreasonably, termed *Toba-e*, Toba pictures. They were first published in printed form in 1720 in a book called *Wakan meihitsu ehon tekagami* (*An Illustrated Handbook of Famous Japanese and Chinese Paintings*). I summed them up in *The Art of the Japanese Book* thus: "The stock comic elements…are the fantastically long, skinny, and acrobatic limbs, and the inanely grinning mouths of the figures in lunatic action."

Hasegawa Mitsunobu was an early exponent of these freakish drawings, and in the book named takes as his themes several quasi-historical events. The one illustrated concerns the attempt of the 12th-century warrior Satō no Tadanobu to fend off his assailants by hurling a *gō* board at them.

the literatus). It sums up all we know of the artist: at various times *sake* brewer, curio dealer, writer of libretti for puppet plays, and painter without school or class distinctions. He was scurrilous, skeptical, and nonconformist.

The old gentleman has been brought to the door of his garden room by the cry of the *hototogisu* (cuckoo-like bird) which seems to have taken off from the calligraphy of the verse at the right.

PLATE 89
MATSUYA JICHŌSAI (active c. 1780–1803)
Three Samurai and a Snail
From ***Ehon kotozugai***
かつらかさね
(meaning obscure)
1805

In their extremest form, *Toba-e* are meaninglessly crazy. In time, sophisticated wits like Jichōsai used what were superficially the same type of figures as described in No. 87 to point up some underlying moral, and even added a scrap of text to reinforce their drift. Jichōsai in particular gives a satirical twist to scenes involving pseudo–*Toba-e* forms, with figures that lie between real flesh and blood and witless zanies.

The three samurai in this specimen are nonplussed, if not scared, by the oversize snail caught in the beam of their lantern.

PLATE 88
MATSUYA JICHŌSAI
Chajin at the Door of his Garden Room
From ***Katsura-kasane***
絵本古鳥図賀比
(meaning obscure)
1803

In this fully color printed book, while not departing from an offhand treatment of the people acting out his scenes, Jichōsai manages to make them seem almost human, and fit accompaniment to the poetical inscriptions. This is a justly famous book, in which the style hovers between *Toba-e,* Osaka genre, and pure *bunjinga* (the art of

89

90

PLATE 90
GOUNTEI SADAHIDE (1807–1873)
Washington
From *Merika shinshi*
米利新誌
(*New Records of America*)
1855

The impingement of the Western world upon Japan in the mid-19th century was an unmitigated shock. For 250 years, Japan had rigorously isolated itself from the rest of the world, Europe and America were like fabled lands known only by clandestinely introduced word and picture, and when Yokohama was opened in 1861 as a port for the disembarkation of the *gaijin* (people from abroad) there was a flood of publications concerning the foreigners and their strange way of life.

The opening of Japan to intercourse with the West had been more or less forcibly initiated by the uninvited visit of an American squadron under Commander Perry in 1853, and by another larger fleet in 1854. In 1855, publication of *Merika shinshi* indicated that opposition to pictures and accounts of foreign lands had ended. The artist is not named, but because of his leading role in designing *Yokohama-e* (Yokohama pictures), Sadahide is believed to have been responsible for this curious compilation, which is probably based on a Dutch original, still not identified.

In 1855, there was very little reliable data available about America, but what the artist lacked in authentic information he was quite equal to supplying from imagination. The city of Washington, for example, is introduced by a very apocryphal view of a street of unlikely buildings and a horse-drawn cab. "All day long," records the text, "streets are never deserted but are always crowded with horse-drawn carriages. It is said that carriages of wealthy people have wheels made of silver. There are bookstores in great numbers in Georgetown. Bread and tobacco are the two products sold in largest quantities in this town."

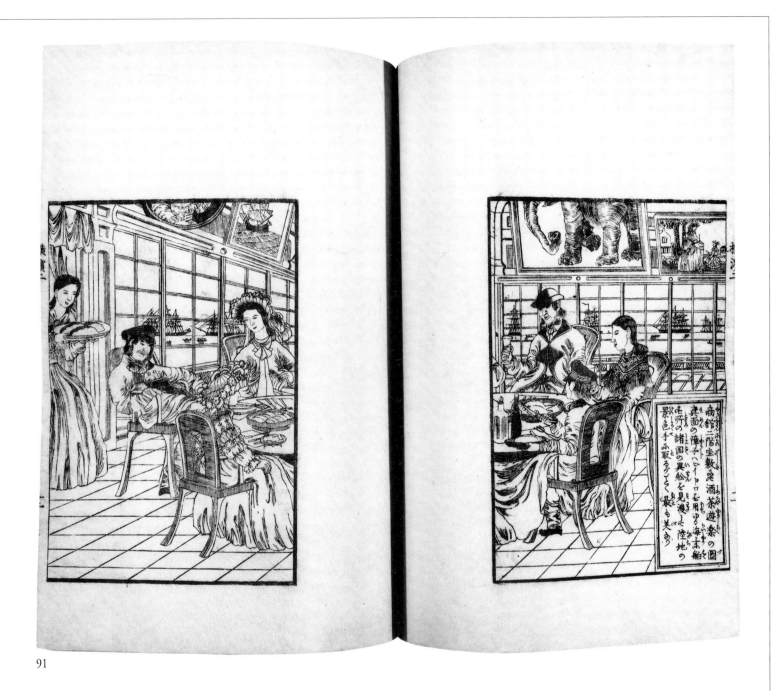

91

PLATE 91
GOUNTEI SADAHIDE
American Family at Table
From *Yokohama kaiko kembushi*
横浜港開見聞誌
(*Observations on the Opening of the Port of Yokohama*). Part I
1862

Another book, this time bearing the signature of Sadahide, was published after the opening of Yokohama as a port. It was brought out over a period, Part I in 1862, Part II three years later. It is a much more believable picture of the invaders, their way of life, their houses and belongings, their black ships. On the whole, Sadahide presents a fairly unfavorable account of the uninvited guests. There was no love lost between them and the natives. To us today, the picture of an American family seated at a meal around a circular table is unexceptional, but the Japanese could not fail to sense the uncouthness of this group of ill-favored foreigners in their outlandish clothes. Even their habit of sitting stiffly in high-backed chairs was brought home. Nor can the invasion fleet be lost sight of through the windows. Throughout the many telling illustrations to this book, Sadahide covertly poses the accusation, "By what right?"

92

PLATES 92–95
NAKAMURA HŌCHŪ (active early 19th century)
Kōrin gafu
光琳畫譜
(*The Drawing Book of Korin*)
1802

R., like many another intent on making his collection as far as possible comprehensive in its coverage, found some books more to his taste than others. His reaction to books of the "Decorative" school was immediately strong, and he found greater pleasure in them than in most others. This again was probably a reflection of an underlying bias in his reception of foreign art to those features that bespeak national characteristics. The aptitude to decorate is universal, of course: in Japan it led to the simplification and modification of natural forms, human as well as all others, of making patterns of such forms and providing color with an eye not to naturalistic accuracy

but to the demands of compelling decor and rhythm. There is a general consensus that this aptitude for decor is of major significance in any study of the aesthetic of Japan.

In books, the first flowering of this flair for apt decoration was in the so-called *Kōetsu-bon* (Kōetsu books), mostly Nō play texts, printed on colored papers and embellished with patterns in silver mica. They were produced in the early 17th century and earned their collective name from the belief that Kōetsu, renowned calligrapher, painter, and potter, was responsible for their design, a supposition possible but without solid proof. *Kōetsu-bon* are rare, and so far, R. has been unable to secure a worthy specimen. He does, however, have a splendid copy of what is generally conceded to be the most truly representative album of Rimpa color prints, the *Kōrin gafu*, designed by Nakamura Hōchū, supposedly after designs or paintings by Kōrin, Kōetsu's most distinguished follower, and published as late as 1802.

The long interval between *Kōetsu-bon* and the *Kōrin gafu* calls for comment. Ōgata Kōrin (1638–1716), profiting by Kōetsu's exam-

93

ple, brought the Rimpa style to its highest expression, but neither he nor his immediate pupils exploited its potential in woodcut form. It was left to his latter-day follower, Hōchū, to achieve what earlier masters, closer to the originator, had declined or failed (through lack of color printing) to attempt. Hōchū entitled his book *The Drawing Book of Kōrin,* but the prints are based on what Hōchū knew of original paintings by Kōrin, and, as with all revivals, he tended to intensify the most prominent characteristics of the originals.

Plate 92
Six Immortal Poets

Six Immortal Poets is a fair example. These are, of course, imaginary portraits. Hōchū had simply used them as human forms that, in fancy Heian getup, could be manipulated into any combination that took his whim. The features of the *Six* are intentionally crude, the

forms anchored around two, one at either side, whose almost feature-less bodies are, above all, weighty.

Plate 93
Fuji and Pines

For any picture of Fuji to be striking it had to transcend a too-well-known image: the bare truth, after so many similar depictions, was not enough. Hōchū, or Kōrin, accentuated the conical shape by drawing it up to a higher and more pointed peak, and confessed to the non-literalism by adding freakish pines, minimal blobs achieved with a full brush. There were certain technical ploys special to Rimpa: submersion of anything like realistic detail, and the resort to *tarashikomi,* a brush technique whereby an addition of moist color to an area already part dry brought about a fusion of pigments quite beyond the strict control of the artist.

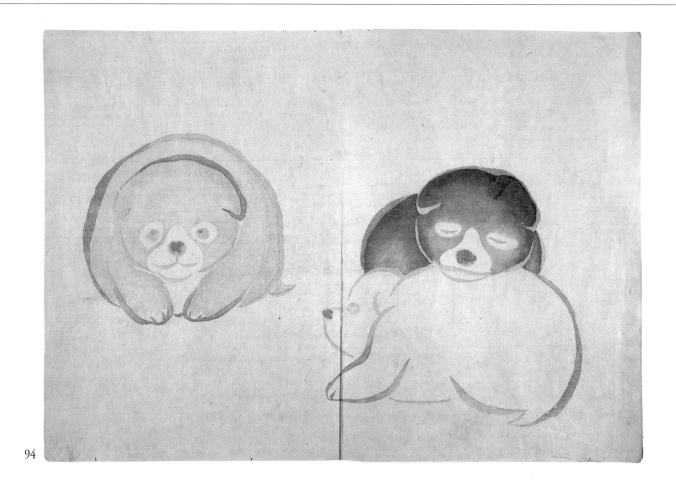

94

95

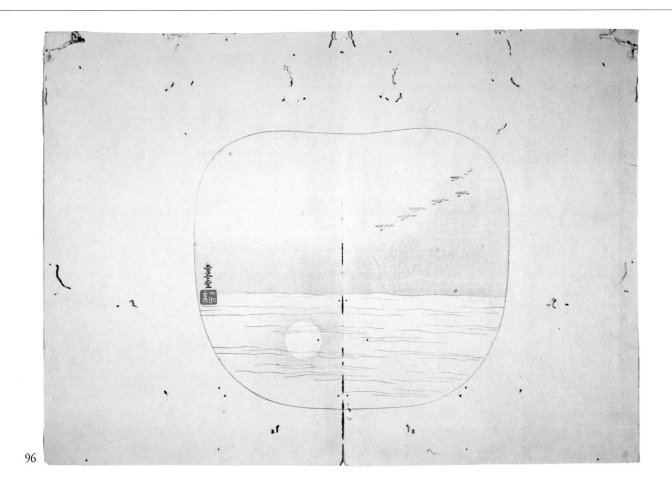

PLATE 94
Three Puppies

People in Japan were liable to become maudlin over defenseless pup-
pies, and great artists like Ōkyo and Rosetsu were among those who
treated them with an unwonted indulgence. Hōchū may have had a
particular example of Kōrin's in mind, but in any case went out of his
way to overplay the whimsy and presented these overfed pets in a
manner that reminds us of Dalí's flabby watches in his well-known
painting.

PLATE 95
Plum Branch

As so often in revivals, an element of caricature is imported, and
Hōchū exaggerates both the asymmetry of pattern and the chance
effects of *tarashikomi* in this striking study of a flowering plum
branch. Apart from Fuji, there is hardly any subject more hackneyed
than this, but Hōchū's print is immediately striking for the decor that
falsity to nature has made possible.

PLATE 96
NAKANUMA SHŌKADŌ (1584–1639)
Fan-Shaped Painting of Skein of Geese and Reflected Moon
From *Shōkadō gajō*
松花堂画帖
(*An Album of Shōkadō's Paintings*)
1804

Shōkadō was, of course, a much earlier painter than Kōrin or Hōchū,
but the album of prints based on his paintings was not published
until 1804, and a number of prints have Rimpa leanings, perhaps
given the slant by reason of the new recognition of the style about
that time. It was a period when the paintings of several great artists of
the past, and of different schools, were being publicized in woodcut
versions: already illustrated are Taiga and Buson in posthumous trib-
utes (Nos. 5–8 and 10).

Shōkadō gajō is a series of evocative woodcuts after Shōkadō's
paintings, more faithful to the originals than Hōchū's after Kōrin, yet
still allowing ample scope to the printmakers to create new works of
art in graphic terms. The fan is especially successful in its simplification and its subtle use, by the printer, of block wiping to achieve
transitory fade-out effects.

97

PLATE 97–98
SAKAI HŌITSU (1761–1828)
Chrysanthemums and Stream and *Irises*
From *Ōson gafu*
鶯邨画譜
(*A Book of Paintings by Ōson*)
1817

Hōitsu was an eclectic artist who is often classified as Rimpa, but who tended to be only half-hearted in his adherence to Rimpa principles. Confining this somewhat heretical criticism to printed works, there are two albums to consider, the *Ōson gafu* (Ōson being one of Hōitsu's studio names) and a sequel (no copy of which is known with a title). These are both very engaging works, full of delightful color prints, but compared with the forthright prints in *Kōrin gafu,* which are sometimes marked by an intentional coarseness or naivete, Hōitsu's seem genteel and even a little tame. Nonetheless, *Irises* makes a beautiful book page.

In the design above, Hōitsu seems to have been more consciously striving to create a truly Rimpa effect, but again he lacks the boldness, the recklessness even, of the committed pattern maker. The chrysanthemums are too realistic and the conventional silver lines of the water give the scene an ambivalence but they do not convert it into a Rimpa abstract.

98

100

PLATE 99
MATSUMURA GOSHUN (1752–1811) and
ANOTHER (unsigned)
Cherry Blossom and Two Hares
From *Gakuga shokei*
学画捷径
(*A Shortcut to the Study of Painting*)
1836

The cherry blossoms here are a very stock design after Goshun, who had, of course, been dead many years; the other page, of two hares, is unsigned but has the unexpected charm and surprise of a netsuke of the 1830s. It is truly, if accidentally, in the Rimpa mold: the animals are stylized; the color, fortuitous; the contrast of blank silhouette with mottled shape is studied. It is, in the end, a playful trifle, but like many other Japanese trifles, a work of real artistry.

PLATE 100
AIKAWA MINWA (died 1821)
Swallows and Willow
From *Kōrin gashiki*
光琳画式
(*Kōrin's Style of Painting*)
1818

Minwa was another artist who admired Kōrin, but judging by his version of the great master, never fully appreciated Rimpa in its extremest form, although coming perhaps closer in a few prints than Hōitsu. The *Swallows and Willow* makes a very decorative print, but its charm is a world away from the quintessential Kōrin.

PLATE 101
SEIZEI KIGYOKU (dates not known)
Waves
From *Kigyoku gafu*
其玉画譜
(*The Drawing Book of Kigyoku*)
1901

Around the turn of the 20th century, the swing to Rimpa, or what has to be termed Neo-Rimpa, became year by year more pronounced. Little is known of Kigyoku, but he had links with earlier masters of decor through his father, who is known to have been a pupil of Suzuki Kiitsu, one of the leading Rimpa painters of the 19th century, but known in books only by uncharacteristic prints.

Kigyoku's style prompted the powerful Kobayashi Bunshichi (possibly the greatest of native Ukiyo-e collectors) to publish this book of designs, and there is no mistaking their debt to Kōrin, or the fact that they have been infected by a modernism that converts them into a new species of design, matched by color that often seems bizarre.

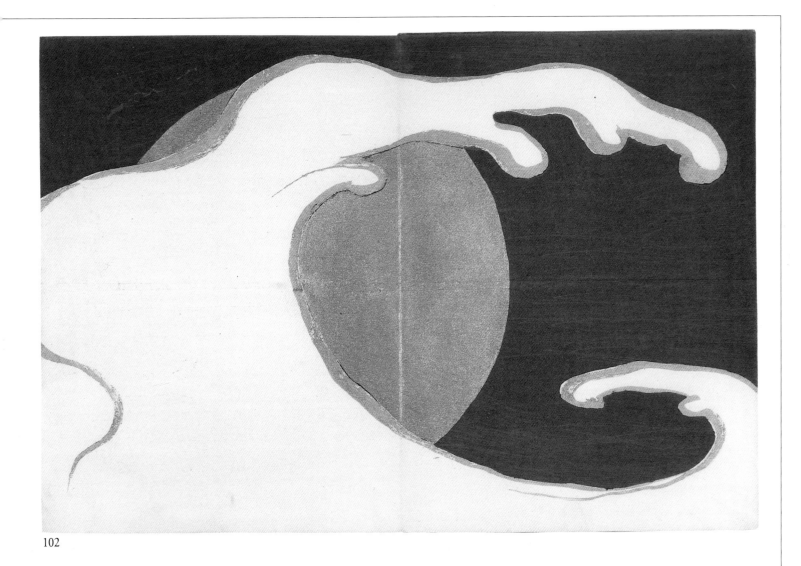

102

KAMISAKA SEKKA (1866–1942)
Momoyo-gusa
百々世草
(*A World of Things*)
1909–1910

Kigyoku, or at least his startling color, prepares us to some extent for Kamisaka Sekka, though Sekka as a print designer is far greater and is a true Neo-Rimpa artist whose works are of such power that they invoke a word like "genius" to describe him. It was through the vision of the publishers Unsōdō that Sekka was given his opportunity to make a name that now stands for all that is exceptional in Rimpa color prints in the early 20th century.

As a painter in the late 19th century, Sekka was a safe traditionalist, rehashing themes that, in a world swiftly changing under the impact of the West, recalled medieval Kyoto in all its glory, and especially the gorgeous color and patterning of costume. Yamada Shinsaburō, head of Unsōdō, which was newly on the publishing scene in Kyoto, perceived how Sekka's style could be the basis of powerful woodcuts and in effect it was he who gradually molded Sekka's approach to the color print medium and honed the techniques of block cutters and printers in his employ to meet his requirements.

The first album showing the emergence of this strong revival of Rimpa was entitled *Chigusa* (*A Variety of Flowering Plants*), and comprised three volumes published in 1899 to 1903. What is looked on as the greatest work in the new genre is *Momoyo-gusa* (*A World of Things*) — first volume, 1909; volumes 2 and 3, 1910. Astonishingly, these sensational volumes had hardly been noticed in the West until a set appeared in a Sotheby's sale in London in 1976. They were immediately acclaimed and have since become as sought after by collectors as other rare masterpieces of Japanese book art.

The prints owe their power to ploys already encountered in *Kōrin gafu* (Nos. 92–95) but carried to their ultimate: exaggerated angle of viewpoint; simplification of forms; violent contrasts of color. Limitation to reproductions of merely three prints can only partially bring home Sekka's originality and fecundity.

PLATE 102
Waves and Sun, vol. 1
1909

Simplification can be carried no further. These are elemental forms: emblems of constancy—the rising sun—and eternal restlessness—the waves.

PLATE 103
Chrysanthemum Boy, vol. 2
1910

The slant of the boy's figure across the sheet and the way it is thrust right to the forefront compel the viewer's attention, and the contrasting color of the boulder and the massed blossoms accentuate the diagonal shaft of the boy's blue outer robe. The fluffy mop of hair is a keynote in the composition and helps to situate the subject in ancient China, scene of the legend. For some minor accident when attendant on the Emperor in about 950 B.C., the Chrysanthemum Boy, was exiled to a place where chrysanthemums abounded. To while away the time, he wrote on chrysanthemum leaves a runic sentence by Shakyamuni which, repeated day after day, ensured safety and longevity.

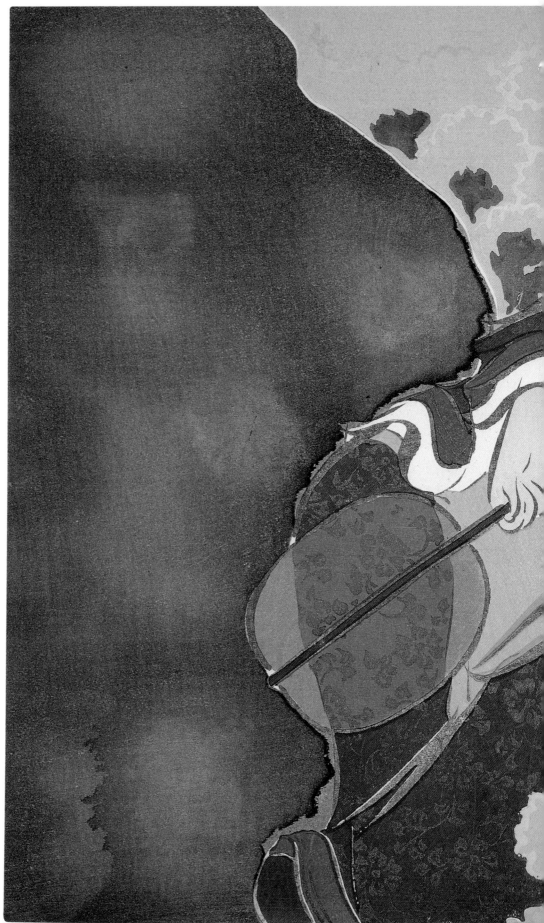

103

PLATE 104
Path Through the Fields, vol. 3
1910

Here the simplification is so extreme that but for the semi-naturalistic figure, it could qualify as a pure abstract, comparable to a painting by Mondrian. The composition revolves around the figure which is just off-center, and so gives the inevitable asymmetry. The almost geometrical grid of the raised paths separates areas of flat color, yellow, green, and pink. In some ways, this is perhaps the most remarkable of all the *Momoyo-gusa* color prints.

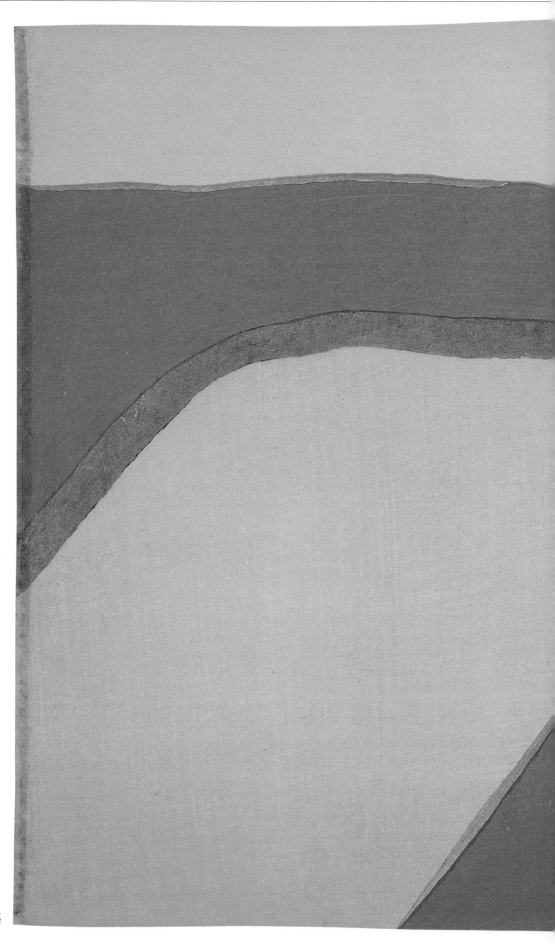

104

105

PLATES 105–106
KAMISAKA SEKKA
A Circlet of Butterflies and
Five Butterflies with Long Antennae
From *Chō senrui*
蝶千種
(*A Thousand Butterflies*)
1903

Before undertaking *Momoyo-gusa,* Unsōdō had given Sekka a commission that was obviously intended to stretch his powers of patterning and his ingenuity to the limit. The book was a series of prints based on butterflies—its title was *Chō senrui* (*A Thousand Butterflies*). It had little to do with the insects known to lepidopterists: they were merely *points de départ* for patterns, and a perfect vehicle for exploitation in woodblock color printing. Some, as in *A Circlet of Butterflies,* are recognizably butterflies; others, further and further away from the norm, become extravaganzas only remotely connected to the natural insect, such as *Five Butterflies with Long Antennae.* One feels that it is more than pure coincidence that Sekka's prints foreshadow the Art Nouveau creations of the great designer Josef Hoffmann. Even if Hoffmann was not directly inspired by this album by Sekka, it was typical of the stream of paintings and prints now reaching the West and leading in ways still not fully understood to the phenomenon we know as Art Nouveau.

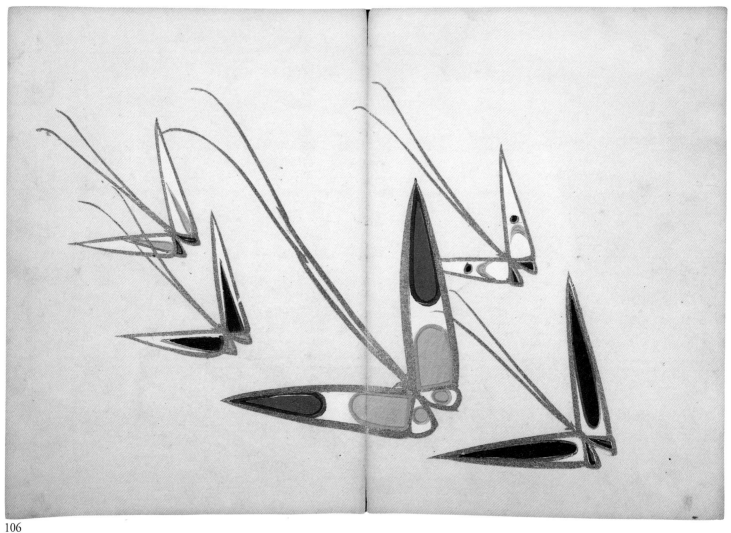

PATTERN BOOKS

During the first three decades of this century, books of color printed patterns, like the *Butterfly* book of Sekka, became increasingly popular. The vogue for kimono pattern books began much earlier, as far back as the 1660s, and by the Meiji period color printing was being lavishly employed for publications concerned with a far wider range than dress alone. Such books had a practical value for designers — of fabric and dress materials, of ceramics, and other articles of domestic use — but by the 20th century they seem to have attracted a growing number of people who found pleasure in collecting albums and textbooks of this nature for their own sake and with no thought for their possible usefulness.

Some designers, like Sekka, soon became notable. Furutani Kōrin was another whose name appears frequently on publications of this kind. No. 109, ingeniously contrived from fern leaves, is one of a volume of patterns entitled *Seika*, 1902; No. 110 the dramatically

bisected fan, is from another of his compilations. But as often as not, the artist is not named, and indeed, was treated as an anonymous artisan. There is little that can be said about the designs reproduced on the following pages (Nos. 107–112) except that they are typical of a positive flood of colorful patterns appearing in various publications, whose titles are often vaguely poetic and even obscure. Unsōdō were frequently the producers of the higher class albums, but other publishers began to specialize, and as a result a surprisingly high proportion of the color-printed books published from 1900 to 1940 were of this type.

To R., the maxim "By their patterns shall ye distinguish between culture and culture" was pertinent to his study of the contrasting societies of mankind, and he has amassed a remarkable number of revealing books of the pattern-book type, warranting more detailed consideration than can be given here.

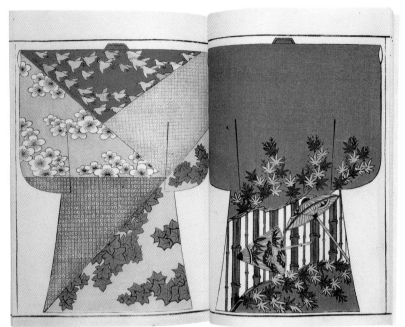

107

PLATES 107–108
ANONYMOUS
Kimono patterns
From *Mōyō hinagata Naniwa no ume*
模様雛形難波の梅
(*Patterns of Osaka Plum Blossoms*)
1885

108

109

110

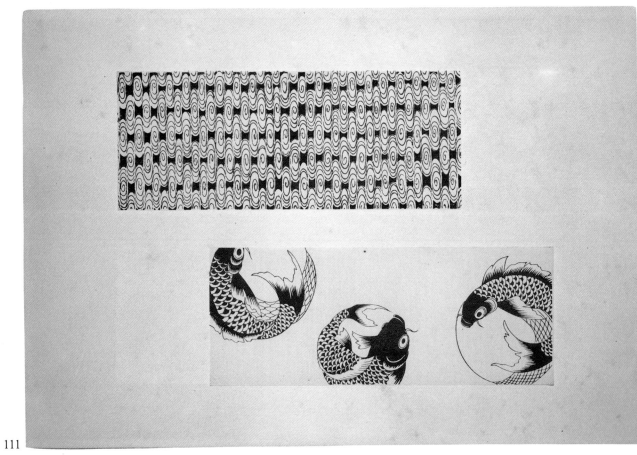

111

113

PLATE 113

YŪZANDŌ (dates unknown)

Orchids (Epidendrum)

From *Yūzandō gafu*

有山堂画譜

(*The Drawing Book of Yūzandō*)

1762

The remaining reproductions in this book up to 118 are loosely brought together under the heading Independents, not because the artists are necessarily so unclassifiable, but because the books they designed fall outside the label of any particular school.

The Yūzandō print comes from a Japanese version of a book originally published in China, and is perhaps a doubtful claimant to a place in a selection from Japanese books. It justifies itself on two grounds: first, all trace of the Chinese original seems to have disappeared; second, it may have inspired the great painter Jakuchū to produce two books and a scroll in a similar technique. In Japan, the "white-line" method was known as *takubon*, "rubbings," or *ishizuri*, "stone print," from the ancient Chinese practice of taking rubbings from carvings on stone, somewhat akin to Western brass rubbings.

The book by Yūzandō (in Chinese, *Youshantang*) was first published in China in 1724, and although, as mentioned above, no copy seems to have survived, a copy of a later Chinese edition is in the British Library. This was produced by normal relief printing, but, repeating the word *shipu*, "stone register" in the title, it proves that the sourcebook was in white reserve on black. There were two volumes—one devoted to bamboos, the other to epidendrums.

The single volume acquired by R. is of epidendrums, and there is no trace of the companion bamboo volume. What makes R.'s book so special is that it bears the seal of Jakuchū, was presumably owned by him, and perhaps persuaded him to employ *ishizuri* in his own printed work. Taken by R. to a symposium on Japanese painting held in New Orleans in 1983, it intrigued and mystified a very erudite and cosmopolitan band of scholars.

The epidendrum, like the bamboo, was often taken by classical artists, Chinese and Japanese, as a subject especially suitable for displaying virtuosity in brushwork. The resource of the block cutter comes over even in the "white-line" technique, with the interweaving of passages of solid white with others that comprise scratchy outlines.

PLATE 114
Itō Jakuchū (1716–1800)
Hypericam chinensis *and a Cricket*
From *Jakuchū gajō*
若中画譜
(*An Album of Pictures by Jakuchū*)
c. 1890s

Jakuchū is one of the few supremely great Japanese artists who (apart from members of the Ukiyo-e school) seem to have been impelled to make essays in graphic art. He elected to project himself by means of an arcane medium, the so-called *ishizuri. Ishizuri*, "stone print," was a misnomer, giving the products a false classical relationship to Chinese rubbings from stone carvings, but achieved by an incredibly difficult process of carving the design on a woodblock, forcing the surface of a sheet of very thin dampened paper into the intaglio areas thus created, and then coating the rest of the sheet on the untouched area of the block with ink, applied by a "dabber," leaving the design in white reserve. However hazardous it was to employ such a method, Jakuchū, with dedicated publishers, produced two books and a long scroll with spectacular results. One no longer spares a thought for the craftsmen who interpreted his designs with such pains: it is the mastery of the designer, the astonishingly decorative and compelling power of the pictures.

The two books, published no doubt in very small editions in 1768, are now known by pitifully few copies spread around the world, and because of the unlikelihood of either ever coming his way, R. was very happy to acquire a copy of the excellent woodblock facsimile (published by Unsōdō, no less), from which the specimen reproduced here comes.

114

PLATE 115
Chō Gesshō
Haiga with Cavorting Plovers
From *Zoku koya bunko*
続姑射文庫
1798

Haiku is a form of Japanese verse much written about, and translations in foreign languages are common. The form limits the number of syllables to seventeen and in that restrictive compass the poet proposes images that become evocative according to the strength of each reader's susceptibility and sympathy.

Haiga are even more esoteric and less familiar outside Japan: in *haiga*, the verse has a pictorial accompaniment, but just as the words are other than descriptive, so the image drawn alongside the calligraphy is not intended to be illustrative, but becomes, as it were, an emanation, matching or reinforcing the mood of the poem.

There are many anthologies of haiku, some with *haiga* among them, but the masterpiece among *haiga* books is unquestionably *Zoku koya bunko* (on which title a dissertation could be written without adding to our enjoyment of the book). In brief, Chō Gesshō, an artist who painted in the Nanga tradition, became the principal artist in a sequel to an earlier anthology, *Koya bunko*, published in 1768, and, by chance almost, discovered an innate aptitude for making this mysteriously creative combination of verse and drawing. The book was in five volumes and Gesshō runs the gamut of what was feasible in an art form he had taken to new heights of expressiveness.

From this vast exposition of *haiga* one example will have to suffice. The poem is by Kikō and says, enigmatically, "A flock of plovers might make the evening moon wet." The joyously abandoned birds, whose aerial acrobatics are so marvelously captured, are no more explicit than the verse, which only hints at the reflection of the moon in the waves, and of the splash of the birds as they brush the water with their wings.

117

115

PLATE 116
KEISAI MASAYOSHI (1764–1824)
Two Pheasants and a Jay
From *Kaihaku raikin zui setsu*
海舶来禽図彙説
(*Commentary on Images of Birds from Overseas*)
1793

Masayoshi was trained by Shigemasa to be an Ukiyo-e artist, and certainly, in the early years of his career, he was true to his calling, illustrating a very large quantity of cheap fiction; but from the mid-1780s he was much concerned with works that are the very antithesis of Ukiyo-e, and he is best classed as Independent.

The first edition of his book of birds, published in 1789, rivals Utamaro's bird book (see Nos. 68–69), and both, in different ways, prove the supreme mastery of the printmakers.

Masayoshi's book implied that the birds were imported from China and the pictures copied by Masayoshi from a Nagasaki artist's originals. To support this fact (or fiction?) the book opens with two prints of Chinese merchants, one with birds in cages. There were two editions in this form, but a third, in 1793, was completely transformed, involving a conversion of the format from album to *ehon*, a re-cutting of the blocks, the omission of the prints of the Chinese traders, and a telescoping of eight sheets, each devoted to a single bird, to four sheets, each picturing two. All three issues are extremely rare, and R. is the fortunate owner of a copy of the third, from which our illustration is taken.

116

鶹禽

鷓鴣

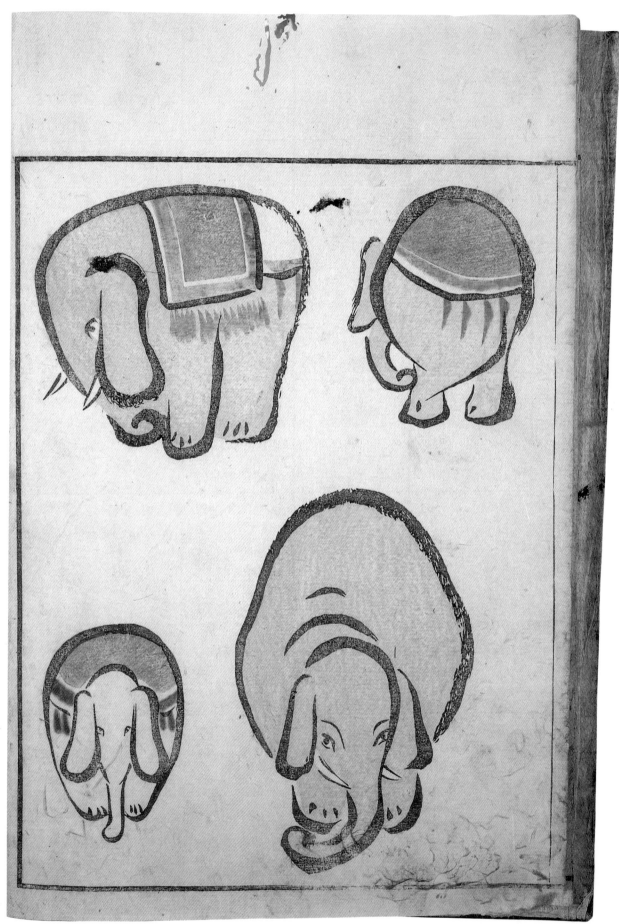

117

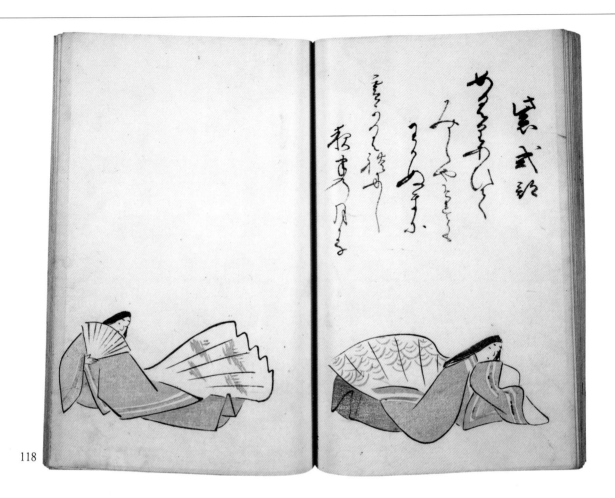

PLATE 117
KEISAI MASAYOSHI
Elephants
From *Chōjū ryakugashiki*
鳥獣略画式
(*Animals and Birds in the Abbreviated Style*)
1797

PLATE 118
KEISAI MASAYOSHI
Two of the
One Hundred Immortal Poets
From *Tenerai hyakunin isshu* (provisional title)
手習百人一首
1815

As an innovator, Masayoshi is chiefly known by his *ryakugashiki* books—a name that describes drawings that are the epitome of brevity: small, witty, expressive, and, above all, simple. For short, we have translated the word as "abbreviated," though it is difficult to find a single word that is adequate. The first volume in this very personal and original style was a book of figures, single or in groups, published in 1795. In 1797 appeared the wonderful book in which equally summary treatment was accorded to animals and birds. *Elephants* demonstrates the broad, unerring brush line with which the animals are concisely set down: the elementary forms, the lugubrious movement, the provision of just enough detail to enable the print-maker to enliven the picture with bright spots of color. The very simplicity of the drawings called for imaginative collusion on the part of the block makers to convert such minimal proposals into solid and amusing decorations to a page.

The *ryakugashiki* style, less miniature and with greater elegance, still informs the portraits of poets in this book, where each figure is isolated on the page to leave space for the owner to inscribe a verse in his own calligraphy above the portrait. (No title label remains on the two recorded copies of the book but the text suggests the provisional title, which indicates that the book was to encourage practice in handwriting.) In R.'s copy, a former owner has dared to interpolate his own brush-drawn verses, and the double page illustrated shows how the amateur has indeed complemented, rather than desecrated, Masayoshi's slight drawings.

119

PLATE 119
AKAMATSU RINSAKU (1878–1953)
Kobe Wharf
From *Hanshin meisho zue*
阪神名勝図絵
(*Sights of Osaka and Kobe*)
1916

It seems right to conclude this selection of prints from Japanese books in the R. Collection with a few from what, for want of a better word, belong to the Transitional period. Much is made by historians of Western art of the influence of Japanese prints on Impressionism and Art Nouveau, but the impact of Western art on the Japanese went deeper than a mere influence: it completely transformed the style of many Japanese artists into something more identifiably Western than Japanese. Of course, it was a gradual process and only

came to full fruition after the turn of the century, but, by 1916, when *Hanshin meisho zue* was published, only the excellence of the woodblock color printing made it impossible not to accept prints, separated from the album itself, as Japanese.

In Akamatsu Rinsaku's *Kobe Wharf* it is not even possible immediately to detect the nationality of the people on the quayside, apart from the kimono-clad woman in mid-distance. The foreign visitors, prominent with their luggage in the foreground, diminish in perspective to the far end of the quay, and ships on the horizon lose their details. Similarly, the clothes of people in the foreground are strongly differentiated, but become more monochrome the greater the distance away. In earlier Japanese views attempting the aerial effects of distance, the perspective was forced and gave Western viewers an uneasy reaction, but Rinsaku handles the situation as perfectly as any French artist of the time.

阪神名勝圖繪 六
甲山 水島瀑布

(版元文淵堂)
(印刷西村)
(刻刻大倉)

120

ASAI CHŪ (1856–1907)
The Photographer and the Frump
and *An Overdressed Couple*
From *Tōsei fūzoku gojūban uta awase*
当世風俗五十番歌合
(*Fifty Modern Genre Scenes Compared in Verse*)
1907

Asai Chū is the archetypal Transitional Japanese artist. A student of one of the earliest Japanese converts to Westernism, Kunisawa Shinkurō (1847–1877), he went on to the as-it-were finishing school in Tokyo under the Italian Antonio Fontanesi, and achieved, in oil paint, a facility that proved, alas, that however closely he followed the Europeans, he would never have anything original to say in this medium. But however much he may have studied Western satiric and comic magazines, he retained in his own prints much of the native spirit of the old books of "moralities," and also of the hilarious color woodcuts that accompanied them. The print of *The Photographer and the Frump* distorts the woman's feet and hands and makes her the butt of the obsequious photographer; in the second print, the dude in loud checks is eyed critically by the lady who is dressed in the worst possible Western taste and has forgotten to change her footwear (*tabi* and *geta*) But the woodblock color printing continues the traditions that prevailed in pre-Westernization days.

121

PLATE 120
MIZUSHIMA NIHOFU (1884–?)
Kabutoyama
From *Hanshin meisho zue*
阪神名勝図絵
(*Sights of Osaka and Kobe*)
1916

In this night scene, the artist has relied on the resourcefulness of the printmakers to create his effect, and so, in conveying with a greater reality than had been normal in Japanese pictures of night, falls back on the medium that in Rinsaku's *Kobe* had been soft-pedaled. In that sense, Nihofu's print is truly Transitional; the woodblock technique was still the means of conveying a non-Japanese realism. In the Edo period, night was suggested by the mere presence of a symbolic lamp, rarely by its beam. Everyone knew the symbol: it was not necessary to drain the picture of light to bring home the prevailing darkness.

PLATE 123
TAKEHISA YUMEJI (1884–1934)
Young Woman Coming Through a Curtain
From *Samisen-kusa*
三昧線草
(*A Story Centered on the Three-Stringed Instrument Called a Samisen*)
1915

Yumeji is another of those artists who, down the centuries, has created the "ideal" female beauty of the age, like Moronobu, Sukenobu, Harunobu, and Utamaro. In the Taishō period (1912–1925) up to the beginning of the Shōwa (1926–1934), Yumeji pictured the type of woman men favored most, creating a type for which we have a counterpart in the West — the woman of the 1920s: indeed, Yumeji's stereotype, with willowy form, mascaraed eyes, and moist rosebud mouth, so much recalls the work of Marie Laurencin that it comes as a surprise to learn that he must have been premonitory to and not a follower of her style. Here, the figure emerging through the parting in the *noren* is in a brilliantly decorated kimono which, like the pale oval face, is thrown into prominence by the solid blue curtain.

123

PLATE 124
TAKEHISA YUMEJI
Sorrowing Woman
From *Konjiki yasha, shūhen*
金色夜叉終篇
(*The Golden Female Demon*). Part I
1920

The wilting young woman who so frequently figures in Yumeji's prints forms a striking image for the cover of the novel *Konjiki yasha*. She kneels in abject misery, her head lowered to the ground, with scattered autumn leaves around her. There is something moving in her unhappiness, unlike the superficial emotions more usually suggested by the artist.

124

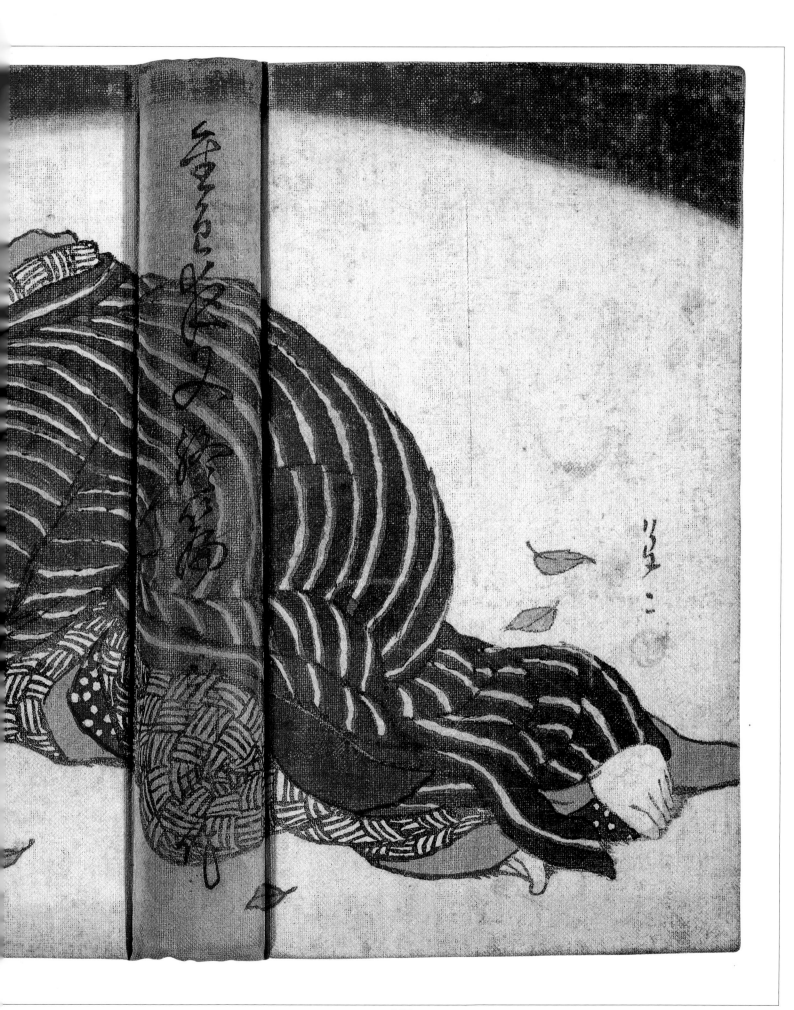

PLATE 125

YOICHIRŌ HIRASE (first half of 20th century)
A Group of Shells
From *Kai senshū*
貝千種
(*One Thousand Kinds of Shell*)
1915

The change that came over books on natural history once Western attitudes had been adopted is exemplified by Hirase's book of shells. Utamaro's glorious book (Nos. 70–71) was a series of prints to adorn a collection of verses, and had little or no thought for scientific presentation. Hirase, in a preface in English, went out of his way to say "this work not being wholly for the benefit of scientific studies…and besides being intended to be distributed not only among our own countrypeople but also friends abroad…I consulted about the printing with the master of the book-store Unsodo, Kyoto, an expert in

printing, who gave warm sympathy and approval to my plan of printing with wood-cuts." And further on, Hirase affirms that "all appreciated the work as a rarity since it, as a whole, represented an elaborate art peculiar to the Japanese."

So, their art now cosmopolitan and widely distributed, the woodblock print was still recognized by the Japanese as "an elaborate art peculiar to the Japanese"; and by their continuing to use the medium in traditional style, the prints had to be seen as traditional. For the artists to break entirely free from the Transitional phase, the whole basis of producing prints from woodblocks had to be revolutionized: the supremely gifted cadre of block cutters responsible for reproducing the drawings of other artists had to be set aside, and in the future, the woodcuts would be cut by the artists themselves: they were to be, in our term, artist-printmakers. To take this causerie, linking a selection of prints from R.'s collection, into this realm of the *sōsaku hanga,* "the creative print," would be to travel far from Japan itself, the real center of R.'s collecting field.

LIST OF EXHIBITIONS

The Ravicz Collection has been exhibited at the following venues:

Cincinnati Art Museum
Cincinnati, Ohio

Clark Humanities Museum
Scripps College
Claremont, California

Craft and Folk Art Museum
Los Angeles, California

Herbert F. Johnson Museum of Art
Cornell University
Ithaca, New York

Honolulu Academy of Arts
Honolulu, Hawaii

IBM Gallery of Science and Art
New York, New York

Los Angeles County Museum of Art
Los Angeles, California

Minnesota Center for Book Arts
Minneapolis, Minnesota

Munson-Williams-Proctor Institute Museum of Art
Utica, New York

Museum of Contemporary Art
Los Angeles, California

Nelson-Atkins Museum
Kansas City, Missouri

New Orleans Museum of Art
New Orleans, Louisiana

Portland Art Museum
Portland, Oregon

Pratt Graphics Center
New York, New York

San Francisco Museum of Modern Art
San Francisco, California

Seattle Art Museum
Seattle, Washington

Setagaya Museum
Tokyo, Japan

Donald Sheehan Gallery
Whitman College
Walla Walla, Washington

Spencer Museum of Art
University of Kansas
Lawrence, Kansas

University of Michigan Museum of Art
Ann Arbor, Michigan

Walker Art Center
Minneapolis, Minnesota

Jane Voorhees Zimmerli Art Museum
Rutgers University
New Brunswick, New Jersey

SELECT BIBLIOGRAPHY

GENERAL

Brown, Louise Norton. *Block Printing and Book Illustration in Japan.* London: George Routledge & Sons Ltd., and New York: E. P. Dutton & Co. 1924.

Chibbett, David. *The History of Japanese Printing and Book Illustration.* Tokyo, New York, and San Francisco: Kodansha International Ltd. 1977.

Evans, Tom and Mary Anne. *The Art of Love in Japan.* London: Paddington Press. 1975.

Hillier, Jack. *The Uninhibited Brush. Japanese Art in the Shijo Style.* London: Hugh M. Moss Ltd. 1974.

———. *The Art of Hokusai in Book Illustration.* London: Sotheby Parke Bernet and University of California Press. 1980.

———. *The Art of the Japanese Book.* London: Sotheby's Publications. 1987.

Holloway, Owen E. *Graphic Art in Japan. The Classical School.* London: Alec Tiranti. 1957.

Michener, J. A. *The Hokusai Sketchbooks, Selections from the Manga.* Rutland, Vt./Tokyo: Tuttle & Co. 1958.

Mitchell, C. H., with the assistance of Osamu Ueda. *The Illustrated Books of the Nanga, Maruyama, Shijo and Other Related Schools of Japan. A Biobibliography.* Revised edition. Los Angeles: Dawson's Book Shop. 1972.

Smith, Lawrence and Jack Hillier. *Japanese Prints: 300 Years of Albums and Books* (exhibition of the Jack Hillier Collection at the British Museum). London: British Museum Publications, Ltd. 1980.

PUBLIC LIBRARIES AND OTHER INSTITUTIONS

EIRE
Chester Beatty Library and Gallery of Oriental Art: *Japanese Illustrated Books and Manuscripts in the Chester Beatty Library,* catalogue by Sorimachi Shigeo. Tokyo, 1979.

FRANCE
Bibliothèque Nationale: *Livres et albums illustrés du Japon réunis et catalogués par Théodore Duret.* Paris, 1900.

GREAT BRITAIN
Victoria and Albert Museum: *Catalogue of Japanese Illustrated Books in the Department of Prints and Drawings* by Leonard G. Dawes. London, 1972.

ITALY
Edouardo Chiossone Civic Museum of Oriental Art: *Ukiyo-e Prints and Drawings from the Early Masters to Shunsho,* catalogue by Luigi Bernardo Brea and Eiko Kondo, translated by Marie McHugh Barisone. Genoa, 1980.

UNITED STATES
Art Institute of Chicago: *Descriptive Catalogue of the Japanese and Chinese Illustrated Books in the Ryerson Library* by Kenji Toda. Chicago, 1931.

New York Public Library: *Catalogue of Japanese Illustrated Books and Manuscripts in the Spencer Collection of the New York Public Library* by Sorimachi Shigeo. New York, 1968; revised and enlarged edition, 1978.

LIST OF BOOKS ILLUSTRATED

LIST OF ARTISTS

ANONYMOUS
匿名の
Plates 107–108, 112

BAIITSU, YAMAMOTO
梅逸山本
Plate 22

BAIKAN, OKADA
梅関岡田
Plate 21

BAIREI, KŌNO
楳嶺幸野
Plates 50–51

BAITEI, KI
楳亭紀
Plates 11–12

BŌSAI, KAMEDA
鵬斎亀
Plates 13–14

BUMPŌ, KAWAMURA
文鳳河村
Plates 35–37

BUNCHŌ, TANI
文晁谷
Plates 20, 44

BUSON, YAHANTEI
蕪村夜半亭
Plate 10

CHINNEN, ŌNISHI
椿年大西
Plates 42–44

CHŪ, ASAI
浅井忠
Plates 121–122

EISHI, CHŌBUNSAI
栄之鳥文斎
Plates 75–76

GESSHŌ, CHŌ
月樵張
Plate 115

GOSHUN, MATSUMURA
呉春松村
Plates 23, 99

HARUNOBU, SUZUKI
春信鈴木
Plates 64–65

HIRASE, YOICHIRŌ
平瀬与一郎
Plate 125

HŌCHŪ, NAKAMURA
仲方中村
Plates 92–95

HŌITSU, SAKAI
抱一酒井
Plates 97–98

HŌJI, MATSUMOTO
奉時松本
Plate 54

HOKUSAI, KATSUSHIKA
北斎葛飾
Plates 77–83

JAKUCHŪ, ITŌ
若冲伊藤
Plate 114

JICHŌSAI, MATSUYA
耳鳥斎松屋
Plates 88–89

KANYŌSAI, RYŌTAI
寒葉斎（凌岱）
Plate 15

KATEN, MIKUMA
華顛三熊
Plate 9

KEINEN, IMAO
今尾景年
Plate 49

KIGYOKU, SEIZEI
其玉青青
Plate 101

KŌRIN, FURUTANI
古谷紅燐
Plates 109–110

KOSHŪ, HATTA
古秀八田
Plate 33

KUNISADA, UTAGAWA
国貞歌川
Plates 85–86

KYŌSAI, KAWANABE
暁斎河鍋
Plate 58